SITES TO SEE

Historical Landmarks in Tulare County

BY ANNIE MITCHELL

COVER DESIGN BY
LINDA HOLLINGSHEAD HOWELL

PANORAMA WEST BOOKS
Fresno, California
1983

Copyright © 1983
Panorama West Books
8 East Olive Avenue
Fresno, California 93728

Library of Congress Catalog Card Number 83-62939
ISBN 0-914330-63-2

All rights reserved.

Manufactured in the United States of America

Contents

INTRODUCTION
v

ACKNOWLEDGEMENTS
v

PART 1
The Butterfield Overland Mail Route
1

Fountain Springs, 4; Tule River, 5; Between Porterville and Visalia, 6; Visalia, 6; Cross Creek, 7; Lindsay, 7.

PART 2
Historic Sites in Visalia and the Northeast Portion of Tulare County
9

Fort Visalia, 11; Camp Babbitt, 14; The Douglass Tree, 17; The First Grist Mill, 19; Visalia's First House, 19; Visalia's First Church, 21; Visalia's First Hotel, 22; Visalia's First Newspaper, 25; Visalia's First Public School, 25; Visalia's First Secondary Schools, 28; Visalia's First Store, 30; Cenotaph, 31; Centennial Tree, 31; Court Houses of Tulare County, 35; Cutler Park, 37; Election Tree and Woodsville, 38; General Grant Tree, 41; The Chicago Tree (General Noble Tree), 43; General Sherman Tree, 45; Ben Harris, 46; Hockett Trail, 47; Hog Wallows, 48; Hospital Rock, 51; Thomas Jacob, 54; Lone Oak Cemetery, 55; Mooney Grove Park, 56; Kaweah Postoffice, 60; Mark Twain Tree, 63; The Pogue Hotel, 64; Rancho de Kaweah, 65; San Joaquin Rolling Mill, 67.

PART 3
Historic Sites in the Southeast Portion
of Tulare County
71

Balch Park, 73; Bartlett Park, 73; Battle Mountain, 75; Bicentennial Tree, 77; Boot Hill, 78; Centennial Stump, 81; Dutch Corners (Ducor), 83; First Orange Trees, 84; Dr. Samuel Gregg George, 86; Hercules Tree, 87; Hollow Log, 88; Indian Rock Basins, 89; Jordan Trail and Jordan Tree, 91; Old Stage Road, 95; Plano, 96; Porterville's First Church, 98; Porterville Flour Mill, 99; Porter Putnam's Home and Store, 103; Soda Springs (Springville), 105; Home of Ina Stiner, 107; Tailholt, 108; Tule River Indian Reservation, 110; Tule River School District, 112; Vandalia, 113; Woodville School, 114; The Zalud House, 115.

PART 4
Historic Sites in the Southwest Portion
of Tulare County
119

Allensworth, 121; Artesian Water and the Tree Ranch, 122; George Stockton Berry, 124; Cartmill House, 126; First Pumped Well, 128; Fremont Trail, 130; Roth's Spur, 132; Smith College, 133; Tulare's First Church, 134; Tulare's First House, 135; Tulare Lake, 136; Tulare Woman's Club House, 138; Zumwalt Park, 140.

PART 5
Historic Sites in the Northwest Portion
of Tulare County
143

Kingston, 145; Mussel Slough Tragedy, 146; Pool's Ferry, 150; Sibley Hotel, 151; Smith's Ferry and Smith Mountain Cemetery, 153; Stone Corral, 155; Traver, 157.

INDEX
160

Introduction

Historical landmarks are either natural objects or man-made objects. Both may be destroyed by the same forces which made them—nature or man.

Interest in the preservation of our California heritage gained momentum during two observances, the 1950 Centennial celebration of California's admission into the Union and the year-long observance of the nation's Bicentennial in 1976. Both events emphasized the need to safeguard the architectural, environmental and historical heritage of the state and nation.

Many landmarks still exist in Tulare County, but, as in all of California, far too many can only be commemorated by plaques.

The Tulare County Historical Society, Daughters of the American Revolution, E Clampus Vitus, the Tulare County Bicentennial Commission, 4-H groups, Boy Scouts, the Tulare City Historical Society and the Kings County Historical Society have placed plaques on many sites in original Tulare County. Other sites still remain to be marked or are worthy of a visit.

Acknowledgements

The acquisition and selection of the maps and pictures used in this publication have taken many years. I want to thank the following people who were so generous with their help: Harold Schutt, Jeff Edwards, Charles Browne, Mervin Fulton, Vera Vincent, Marge Toledo, Dawrence Glenn and Alan George.

I especially want to thank William Jordan for the map of the Jordan Trail and Floyd Otter for his map of all the early trails over the mountains of eastern Tulare County.

A.R.M.

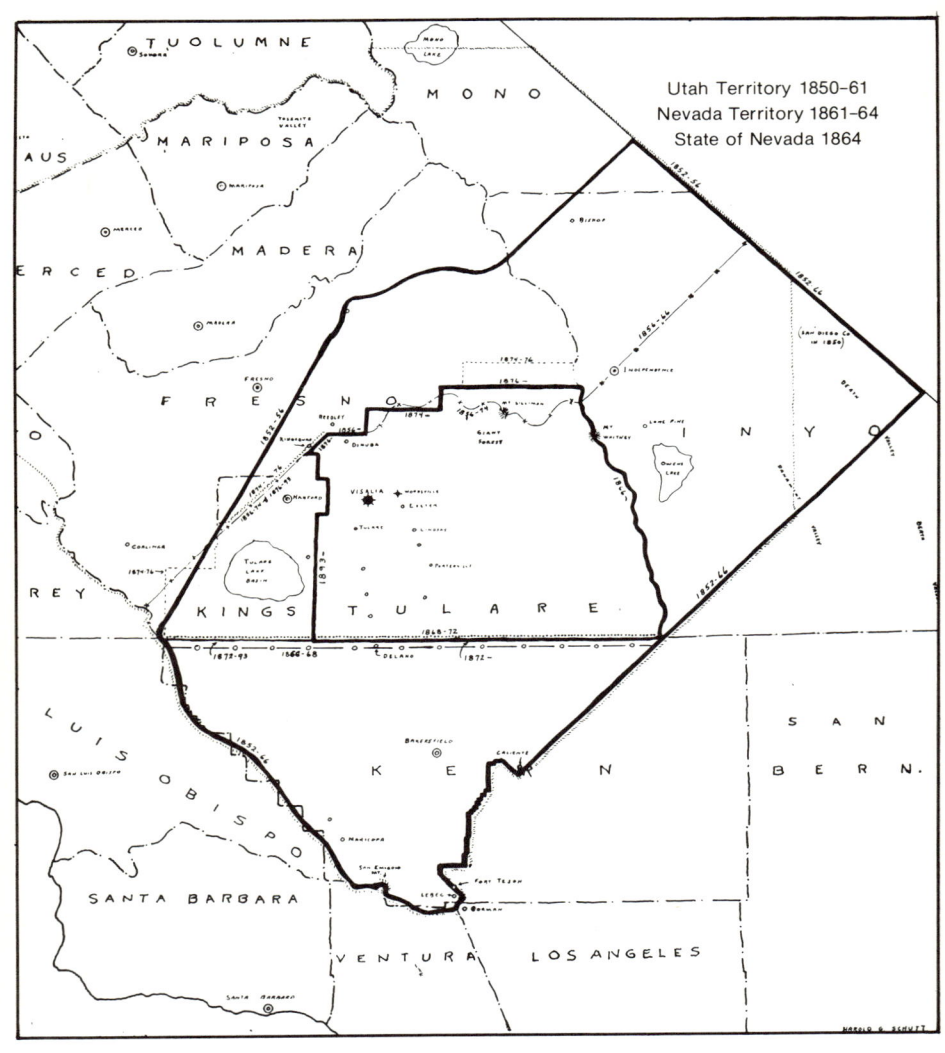

When first organized, in 1852, Tulare County included most of Kings County and much of Fresno, Inyo and Kern counties, as shown on this map. Boundaries were shifted and new counties formed between 1852 and 1893. Since 1893 there has been no change in the Tulare County boundary.

Part 1
The Butterfield Overland Mail Route

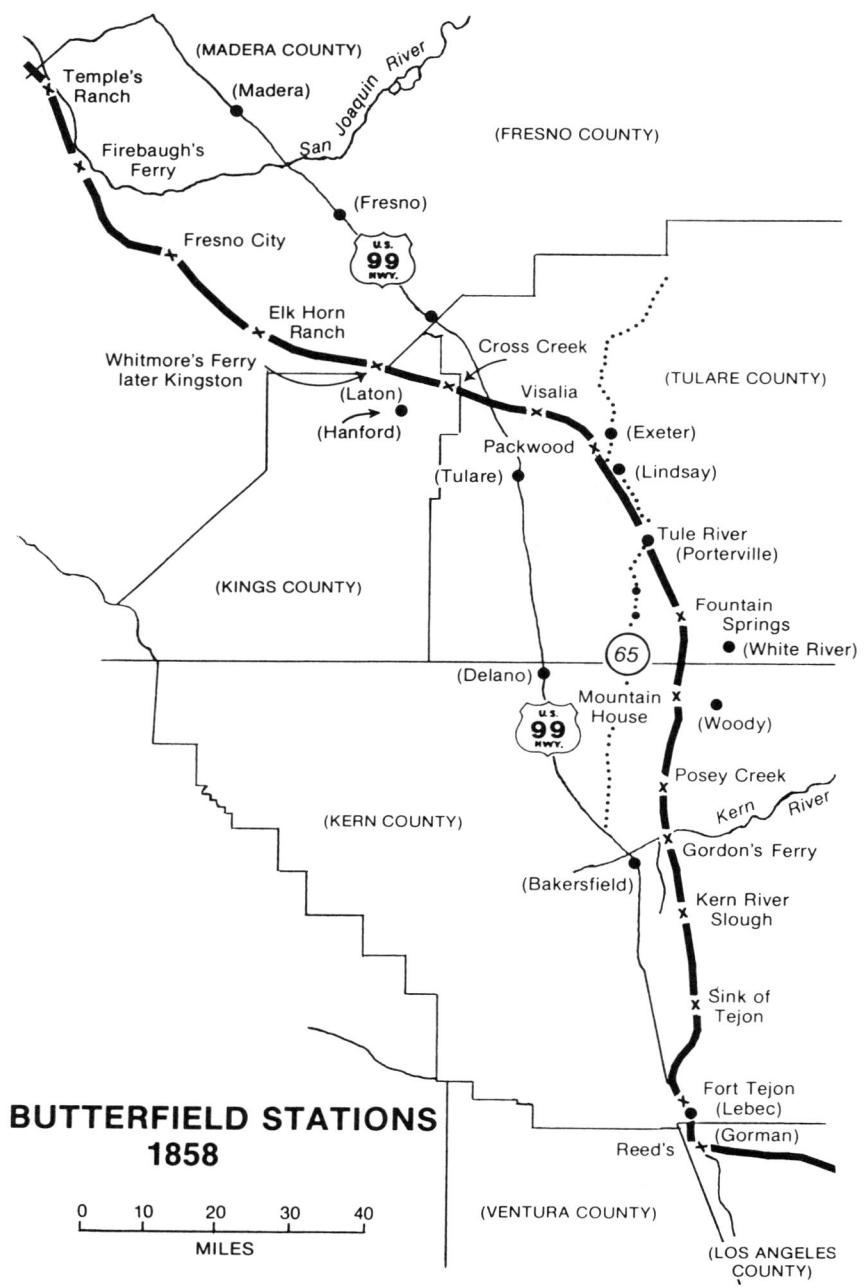

The Butterfield Overland Mail Route

Communication in the pioneer west was expensive, frustrating and uncertain. When Tulare County was organized in 1852, Stockton was the nearest post office. In bad weather it took about a month to make the round trip on horseback. The first post office in Tulare County was granted to Woodsville, October 12, 1853. On June 2, 1855 it was moved to Visalia.

All transportation was slow and hazardous. Californians clamored for better wagon roads, mail service, and a transcontinental railroad. The Pony Express, the Union Pacific and Central Pacific railroads and the Butterfield Overland Mail emerged from these demands.

John Butterfield obtained a federal overland mail contract in 1857. The yearly subsidy was $600,000, and a route through the southern states was selected. Service was to be semi-weekly between Saint Louis and San Francisco. The contract stipulated that the trip had to be made in twenty-five days or less.

Butterfield was a master planner and within a year he had built stations along the 2,795-mile route, bought 1,500 head of stock, wagons and coaches, and had hired drivers and hostlers. One-third of the stations were in California. Seventeen of those were in the central valley and six were in Tulare County. Stations were about twenty miles apart and teams were changed at each station.

Very little comfort was provided for passengers, who were advised to bring a rifle, a revolver, ammunition and a sheathed knife. The fare was $200 and the passenger provided his own food. The mail had to get through on time, and the drivers' slogan, "Gallop, Gulp, and Go," was extremely realistic.

Stages left both terminals September 16, 1858. The westbound coach reached San Francisco in twenty-three days and twenty-three hours. There was one passenger, William Ormsby, a reporter for the *New York Herald.*

The route through the lower valley followed much of the old east side Indian trail. The first valley station was Fort Tejon. The route then went on to Sink of the Tejon, to Gordon's Ferry on Kern River, and to Posey Creek, twenty-six miles northward.

Mountain House on White River was the next stop. Ormsby's report on that part of the trip reads, "The road winds with abrupt turns which keep a team traveling like horses in a circus ring, although the curves are alternately to the right or left or to a hill top."

FOUNTAIN SPRINGS

The Fountain Springs station predated the Butterfield stages. An inn and stage stop were there before 1855, since the springs were at the junction of the Stockton-Los Angeles Road and the road to the White River and Kern River mines. State Registered Landmark Number 648 was placed near that junction in 1958. The wording explains the confusion over the location.

Butterfield Stage Station marker at Fountain Springs east of Ducor at intersection of Avenue 56 (J22) and the Old Stage Road.

FOUNTAIN SPRINGS

ONE AND A HALF MILES WEST OF THIS POINT THE SETTLEMENT OF FOUNTAIN SPRINGS WAS ESTABLISHED BEFORE 1855. IT WAS AT THIS JUNCTION OF THE STOCKTON-LOS ANGELES ROAD AND THE ONE TO THE KERN RIVER MINES. FROM 1858 TO 1861 FOUNTAIN SPRINGS WAS A STATION ON THE BUTTERFIELD OVERLAND STAGE ROUTE.

PLAQUE PLACED BY THE CALIFORNIA STATE PARK COMMISSION IN COOPERATION WITH THE TULARE HISTORICAL SOCIETY.
SEPTEMBER 28, 1958

TULE RIVER

The station on Tule River also predated the Butterfield route. Peter Goodhue had an inn on Scenic Hill in Porterville as early as 1854. Today that inn would be at the intersection of Main Street and Sunnyside Avenue. At that time the Tule River flowed past that location but the flood of 1862 moved the channel southward to its present location. The marker is on the original site.

Butterfield Stage Station marker at Tule River. The marker is in a small park at the intersection of North Main Street and Sunnyside Avenue in Porterville.

TULE RIVER STAGE STATION

HERE PETER GOODHUE OPERATED AN EMIGRANT TRAIL STOPPING PLACE ON THE BANK OF TULE RIVER FROM 1854 UNTIL THE RIVER CHANGED ITS COURSE IN 1862. THIS BECAME A BUTTERFIELD OVERLAND MAIL STAGE STATION, 1858-1861. IT WAS KEPT IN 1860 BY R. PORTER PUTNAM WHO IN 1864 FOUNDED PORTERVILLE, NAMED FOR HIM.

HISTORICAL LANDMARK NO. 473
CALIFORNIA STATE PARK COMMISSION

BASE FURNISHED BY THE TULARE COUNTY HISTORICAL SOCIETY AND GRAND PARLOR NATIVE DAUGHTERS OF THE GOLDEN WEST. PARK ESTABLISHED BY THE CITY OF PORTERVILLE. DEDICATED OCTOBER 11, 1953.

BETWEEN PORTERVILLE AND VISALIA

The station between Porterville and Visalia had three different names. On the timetable it was listed as Packwood Station. Locally it was called either the Pike Lawless Station or the Lone Cottonwood Station. It was about three miles west of present Strathmore, but its exact location has never been determined.

VISALIA

Butterfield Stage Station marker in Visalia is located in front of 116 East Main Street.

Visalia was an important timetable station housed in the Exchange Hotel on the northeast corner of Main and Court streets. The horses were stabled in a corral across the street. On the first trip, Ormsby reported that the stage left Fort Tejon at 4:33 A.M. on October 8 and arrived in Visalia on time at 11:30 that night. He was enthusiastic about the reception given to the driver, himself, and the rapid arrival of mail and newspapers. From then on, stages arrived in Visalia regularly on Tuesdays and Fridays at 11:30 P.M. and left on Wednesdays and Saturdays at 5:00 A.M.

In 1952 the station was marked with a plaque by the Visalia Centennial Committee. The arrival of the stage was re-enacted at 11:30 at night. A copy of the *New York Herald* was read, and Ormsby would have been astounded to know that it was printed that day and flown to Visalia for the ceremony.

In 1973 the Jim Savage Chapter, E Clampus Vitus dedicated an imposing marker at the site of the station. The inscription reads:

> BUTTERFIELD OVERLAND MAIL
>
> AT THIS PLACE, NEAR MIDNIGHT OCT. 8, 1858, VISALIANS GREETED WITH AN ANVIL SALUTE, THE FIRST COACH OF THE PIONEER LINE TO ARRIVE FROM ST. LOUIS. THE VISALIANS' HEARTY WELCOME CAUSED THE ONLY "THROUGH' PASSENGER TO REMARK, "THEY OUGHT TO BE REMEMBERED IN THE HISTORY OF THE TOWN, SO I HEREBY IMMORTALIZE THEM."
>
> JIM SAVAGE CHAPTER 1852
> E CLAMPUS VITUS
> OCTOBER 14, 1973

CROSS CREEK

Cross Creek was the station northwest of Visalia. The site had been in use as a halfway house between Visalia and Whitmore's Ferry since 1855. From Cross Creek the stations were Whitmore's Ferry on Kings River, Elkhorn, Fresno City (present Tranquillity), Firebaugh's Ferry and Gilroy. The trip through the lower valley took forty-one hours.

LINDSAY

There is one more plaque marking the Butterfield stage route. It is State Registered Landmark Number 471 west of Lindsay at the junction of Highway 65 and the Lindsay-Tulare Highway.

> BUTTERFIELD OVERLAND MAIL ROUTE
>
> THIS ROUTE FOLLOWING AN EARLIER EMIGRANT TRAIL WAS LAID OUT IN THE 1850'S AS PART OF THE STOCKTON-LOS ANGELES ROAD. IT WAS USED BY THE BUTTERFIELD OVERLAND MAIL STAGES BETWEEN ST. LOUIS AND SAN FRANCISCO FROM 1858 TO 1861. THIS WAS THE FIRST OVERLAND MAIL OPERATED ON A REGULAR SCHEDULE.
>
> CALIFORNIA REGISTERED LANDMARK #471
> PLAQUE PLACED BY THE CALIFORNIA STATE PARK COMMISSION IN COOPERATION WITH THE TULARE COUNTY HISTORICAL SOCIETY. SEPTEMBER 18, 1958.

Butterfield Stage Station marker west of Lindsay at the intersection of Highway 65 and Highway 137.

Part 2
Historic Sites in Visalia and the Northeast Portion of Tulare County

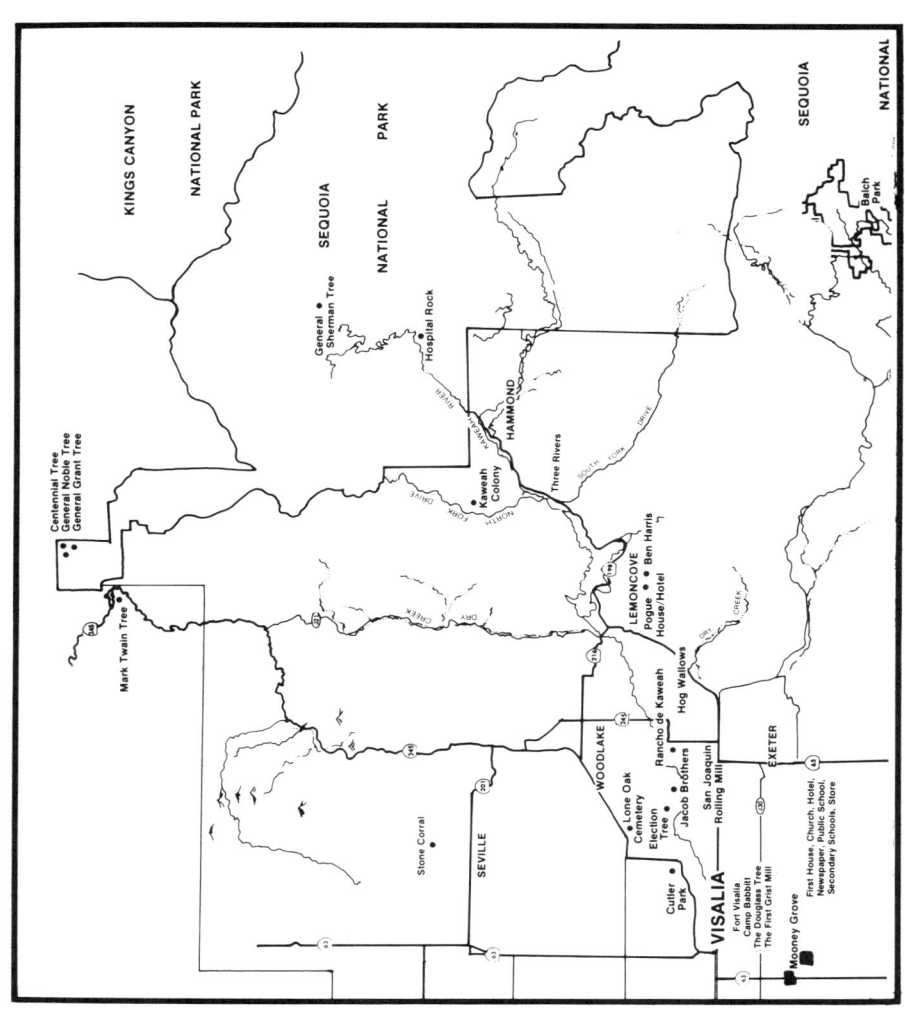

Historic Sites in Visalia

FORT VISALIA

In 1952 Visalia, "The Centennial Queen of the San Joaquin," observed its centennial. During the year-long celebration thirteen markers were placed by the Centennial Committee. Visalia is the oldest town between Stockton and Los Angeles, so each marker commemorates a "first" for the lower valley.

When the first large group of settlers came to Tulare County in 1852, they by-passed the county seat of Woodsville. They came west down a creek for about eight miles, then camped in the heart of the great oak forest. Hundreds of Indians lived in the forest, so the settlers built a stockade in which they could spend the winter. Today that site is bounded approximately by School, Oak, Bridge and Garden streets. No better description of Fort Visalia can be made than to quote from a letter written by Edgar Reynolds, who lived in the fort.

> On the 18th day of April 1852, in company with my three uncles, Reuben, Osee, and Warren Matthews and their families, I left Red Rock, Iowa with an ox team for California. Many little incidents happened before we reached Stockton on the 12th of September. There we lay resting up and on the 12th of October we started for the Four Creeks country as it was then called, landing at Woodsville. Here we stayed for a few days looking around. Then we moved down and camped on the creek just above where Visalia now stands. We cut and piled up a log pen and put our tents in it which the families occupied while the men slept in the wagons. We stood guard at night as the Indians were plentiful.
>
> Soon we commenced to build a fort on the north side of the creek where Visalia now stands. We dug a trench about three feet deep and set up puncheons so the Indians could not shoot through. The fort extended out about four feet at each corner with a porthole so we could rake the sides in case the Indians wanted to climb over. We then built a log house in each corner and was nicely fixed.

It is impossible to list everyone who might have lived in the fort, but old documents, letters and interviews have yielded this list of Tulare County pioneers:

Dr. Reuben Matthews and family	Richard Glenn and family
Samuel C. Brown	Alexander Glenn and family
Abram Murray and family	Calhoun Roberts
	Nathan Baker
Osee Matthews and family	Thomas Baker and family
Warren Matthews and family	John Keener and family
	Robert Stevenson and family
J. S. Mickley	George Ship
Richard Chatten	Garrett Street
Nathaniel Vise	Dr. John Cutler
Thomas Willis	Early Lyons
	Edgar Reynolds

During the winter the fort-dwellers organized a church and a school within the fort. Life in the fort confines was not uneventful, for people faced the task of starting a new community. Most of the men were cattlemen, but there were also lawyers, doctors and merchants. The Matthews brothers were millers and had equipment for a grist mill. Nathan Baker started a general store south of the fort. Samuel Brown built the first house outside the fort.

Romance also came to the fort when three Glenn sisters married. Louisa Glenn married William J. Campbell, Margaret Glenn married Richard Chatten, and Rebecca Glenn married John Patterson.

Nathaniel Vise gave his name to Visalia. He was an eccentric fellow who opened a restaurant in San Francisco in 1852. He featured bear meat on the menu and advertised as "Nat Vise, alias the Bear Hunter." Just what he was doing in the Four Creeks is a matter of conjecture, but he did vote in the organization election of Tulare County on July 10, 1852. He surveyed a parcel of land but never filed on it. He was restless and did not stay in one location very long. He had settled his family in El Monte in 1850 and had restaurants in both San Francisco and San Diego. At various times he was a preacher, horse trader and

The first settlers of Visalia lived within this "fort" during the fall and winter of 1852–53. Today it would be within an area bounded by Oak, Center, Garden and Bridge streets. Standing behind the marker is Alan George, president of the Tulare County Historical Society. The man on the right is unidentified.

fur agent, and in Tulare County he was a land promoter. On November 1, 1852, Vise and O'Neil let it be known that they "had located and surveyed a new town called Visalia, in the finest part of the Four Creeks."

Different explanations have been given for the origin of the name Visalia. Research reveals that Nat Vise came from Visalia, Kentucky, named for his family. He gave the same name to his new town.

Nat Vise did not stay in Visalia for long. He returned to southern California and worked for a fur company. In that job he traveled to the eastern states several times. In 1882 he was staying in Texarkana when the town was hit by a tornado. He took refuge in a brick building which collapsed, killing those inside.

In 1981 a marker was placed on the site of Fort Visalia. The plaque reads:

FORT VISALIA

PIONEER SETTLERS BUILT A LOG STOCKADE IN THIS BLOCK. IT MARKED THE BEGINNING OF VISALIA.

MT. WHITNEY COUNCIL
BOY SCOUTS OF AMERICA

TULARE COUNTY HISTORICAL SOCIETY

FEBRUARY 8, 1981

CAMP BABBITT

California came into the Union in 1850 as a free state. Millions of dollars of California's gold poured into the national treasury during the Civil War. However, large sections of extremely strong anti-Union sentiment existed in the state. Secession was discussed openly in such places as El Monte, Visalia and the mining camps on the Kern and White rivers. It was no secret that men slipped over the mountain passes and trails in Tulare County to join the Confederate Army. A federal undercover agent reported so much "secesh" sentiment in Tulare County that officials felt it necessary to establish a military camp in Visalia.

On October 8, 1862, soldiers of Company D Second California Cavalry arrived in Visalia. Union men mustered a small brass band to welcome the soldiers, but rebel yells and hurrahs for Jefferson Davis drowned out the music.

Colonel George Evans selected a site for the military camp about a mile north of Main Street. He named it Camp Babbitt for the quarter master general of the Pacific. Evans bought flour at five dollars per 100 pounds, barley at two cents a pound, hay from twenty to twenty-five dollars a ton, wood from three to four dollars a cord, and beef at five cents a pound. He emphasized that he bought only from loyal Union men.

Companies I and E arrived later. During the existence of the camp, troops came and went. They traveled back and forth to Owens Valley over both the Hockett and Jordan trails, guarding Tejon Pass and other mountain passes and trails. They fought Indians in Owens Valley and helped track the Mason-Henry guerrilla gang.

Visalia was never declared off bounds, and trouble was inevitable. When the soldiers drilled they were treated to jeers and rebel yells. There were saloon brawls. The soldiers arrested prominent citizens, including State Senator Thomas Baker, took them to the guard house and released them only when they took an oath of allegiance to the Union.

The first murder happened a month after the soldiers arrived. A brawl started in the Fashion Saloon and a bartender shot a soldier. No arrests were made, but the camp commander sent this frantic and exaggerated message to San Francisco: "This command does not number more than 100 men and the rebels can bring against it 250 men in 24 hours and 400 men in 2 days all of them well armed."

The *Equal Rights Expositor* was established in 1862 in Visalia. The newspaper contained such vitriolic editorial denunciations of Lincoln and the Union that it was barred from the mail. Southern sympathizers, many of them women, delivered the newspaper to subscribers. In March 1863 an editorial called the soldiers "base cowards with hearts of does and rabbits." That night the office of the *Equal Rights Expositor* was methodically wrecked. No arrests were made.

A few weeks later, James Wells, a Visalia merchant, was going home when soldiers taunted him about his secesh politics. In the

Camp Babbitt was used from 1862 until the end of the Civil War. The first location was at the southwest corner of Bridge and Race streets. The second site was east of the intersection of the Ivanhoe Highway and Ben Maddox Way.

resulting melee, Wells shot and killed a soldier. That night soldiers hauled a small field piece into Visalia, battered down Wells' house and burned the contents. Meantime Wells' friends smuggled him out of town and eventually into Mexico. He returned later, was tried and acquitted.

In 1865 Camp Babbitt was moved from what is now the 400 block of East Race Street to a site slightly east of the intersection of Ben Maddox Way and East Houston Avenue. Distance did not prevent further brawls and shootings.

Nevertheless there was a pleasant side to life in the camp. The soldiers organized a band, gave concerts, observed national holidays and invited the community. In turn the soldiers were invited to community events and to meals and parties in private homes.

When the Civil War ended, Camp Babbitt was disbanded. As the years passed, sharp differences faded except at election times.

Many years passed before Republicans won election to county or other political offices. Finally, in 1887, Confederate General Tyree Bell, receiver of the Visalia Land Office, persuaded Visalians to observe Decoration Day as a unified community. At last, the Civil War was over in Tulare County.

THE DOUGLASS TREE

Visalia is known as the "City of Beautiful Trees." The valley oak is used for a logo by commercial, professional and civic organizations. A city ordinance protects oak trees and urges residents to plant trees to replace those which must be uprooted because of disease or location. In 1981 the City and the Visalia Chamber of Commerce sponsored an "acorn planting." Citizens collected more than 15,000 acorns and planted thousands of them.

In the 1952 Centennial year, the committee wanted to mark an oak planted when Visalia was young, preferably within the original townsite. The committee found no large oak tree in that area, but selected a tree because its planting date was known.

David R. Douglass built his house on the northwest corner of Willow and Garden streets in 1860. That same year he planted a eucalyptus tree on the east side of the house. The Centennial Committee chose this eucalyptus as a symbol of early Visalia. The Douglass house was moved when the Visalia Community Convention Center was built in 1972, but care was taken not to damage the huge tree. It now stands in the courtyard of the Center where it is symbolic of the vitality of the pioneers.

In 1860 David R. Douglass built a house on the northwest corner of Willow and Garden streets. He planted a eucalyptus tree the same year. Today it is within the courtyard of the Visalia Convention Center.

THE FIRST GRIST MILL

The Matthews brothers, millers from Iowa, brought their mill equipment with them when they came to Tulare County in 1852. Family tradition relates that at least one of the brothers had been in the Four Creeks before 1852. They selected a site for their mill southeast of Fort Visalia. The approximate location of that site today would be the intersection of East Main and Santa Fe streets.

The Matthews brothers hired Indians to dig the mill race and a ditch, which diverted water from the creek to provide irrigation for a corn patch—the first diversion of irrigation water in the lower valley.

Grist mills were essential for pioneers. Corn or wheat was ground for meal or flour, and rolled oats and bran were produced for cattle and poultry food. The usual fee for grinding corn or wheat was seventy-five cents per 100 pounds or a third of the finished product. The 1860 census shows that the Matthews mill was taking in 20,000 bushels of grain or corn a year.

Over the years the mill changed ownership many times, burned several times and was rebuilt. When it burned in 1967 it was razed and not rebuilt.

The first mill has left a permanent legacy for Visalia—the creek running through Visalia is Mill Creek. The principal east-west street was called Mill Street until it was changed officially to Main Street in 1890.

In 1974 the mill site was leveled to make way for new buildings. Workers unearthed two of the original mill stones. One fell to pieces but the second was lifted successfully and transported to the Tulare County Museum in Mooney Grove.

VISALIA'S FIRST HOUSE

In the spring of 1853 Samuel C. Brown built the first house in Visalia. It was a log cabin at what today is the northwest corner of Oak and Court streets.

Mr. Brown was a graduate of Oberlin College with a degree in law. He was admitted to practice in Woodsville on July 6, 1853. His appointment as district attorney soon afterwards marked

In 1853 Samuel C. Brown built the first house outside Fort Visalia. Today it would be located on the northwest corner of Oak and Court streets. The house on the left side of this picture is the house the Browns built on the same site many years later. The large building in the center of the picture is the Tipton Lindsey School. Today the Visalia-Tulare County Library occupies the same site.

the beginning of a long and distinguished legal career that would make him known throughout California.

The original cabin was taken down in 1871 and replaced with a brick structure that was also razed within a few years. The third structure on the same site, a two-story building which was truly a mansion, became the musical center of Visalia, for the Brown daughters were all talented musicians.

The house had five bedrooms upstairs. Downstairs there was a library, sitting room, dining room, kitchen, conservatory, and a large entrance hall extending upward to the roof. The home with its lovely garden stood until 1936, when it was razed.

VISALIA'S FIRST CHURCH

The Methodist Episcopal Church South was organized in 1852. The first church building was constructed in 1857. It would be located today on the west side of Church Street between Acequia and Main streets.

Visalia's first church was organized in 1852 by the Reverend O. P. Fisher and Mr. Christianson of the Pacific Coast Conference of the Methodist Episcopal Church South. For five years the members met in homes or, if the weather was pleasant, in the oak grove.

In 1857 James Persian financed a church building on the west side of what is now Church Street between Main and Acequia streets. It was a two-story brick building and was soon referred as the Brick Church. The upper story was leased to Dr. John Webb, who used it for his office. When the church was not in use by the Methodists, other denominations held services there.

The building was damaged in the flood of 1862 and had to be condemned after the flood of 1868. In 1872 a new church was built on the northeast corner of North Court and School streets.

In 1857 the Reverend John McKelvey organized the First Methodist Church in Visalia. The members met in homes, the Brick Church or the Baptist Church until 1867, when a church was built on the corner of Williow and South Court streets.

Methodism had split nationally before the Civil War actually began. In 1939 the schism was healed and the Visalia churches joined together as the Visalia United Methodist Church. In 1952 a new church was built at 1300 West Main Street. It was dedicated by Bishop D. H. Tippet, a century after Methodism first came to Visalia and the lower valley.

VISALIA'S FIRST HOTEL

The Visalia House was built in 1859 on the northeast corner of Main and Church streets by Dr. William Davenport. This two-story hotel was made from bricks burned in the Visalia Brick Yard. From time to time additions and alterations were made. Dr. Davenport leased the hotel to others.

The first floor included a restaurant, a saloon and offices. The upper story, originally just a big room where men slept on their bed rolls, was later partitioned into bedrooms.

John Crowley bought the hotel and in 1879 sold it to Langston Johnson of Visalia. In 1916 his son, J. Sub Johnson, tore down the Visalia House and built Hotel Johnson. That five-story brick

The Visalia House was built in 1859 and was used until the Hotel Johnson, shown on the next page, was built on the same site in 1916. Hotel Johnson was gutted by a fire in 1968. Both structures were located on the northeast corner of East Main and Church streets.

hotel became one of the best known hotels in the valley. There were sample rooms for drummers, a large dining room, a banquet room, a spacious mezzanine, a large lobby and comfortable bedrooms. Like so many of its predecessors, Hotel Johnson was gutted by a fire in 1968. Today the site is the home of the Main Street Branch of the Bank of America.

Hotel Johnson.

VISALIA'S FIRST NEWSPAPER

The first newspaper in the lower valley was the *Tulare County Record and Fresno Examiner*, issued in Visalia June 25, 1859. Isaac W. Carpenter, owner and publisher, printed a policy statement in the first issue:

> It was a journal for the people: devoted to news, miscellany, agriculture, and to the local interests of Tulare and Fresno Counties. The organ of no party, independent on all subjects. Published every Saturday at Visalia. Uses Overland Mail Route from St. Louis to San Francisco. Office in the front basement of the Courthouse.

In a few weeks Mr. Carpenter sold his newspaper to John Shannon, a well-known California newspaper man. Shannon changed the name to *Visalia Weekly Delta* and openly advocated the doctrine of states' rights.

On September 8, 1860, a rival paper, *The Visalia Sun*, began publication. The man who wrote its editorials was a Visalia attorney, William G. Morris. Shannon and Morris began to write editorials that not only aired their political differences but also became personally libelous.

Morris challenged Shannon to a duel which did not take place. Instead, they began a fist fight which had a tragic ending when Morris drew his gun, shooting and killing Shannon.

The Visalia Sun stopped publication but the *Delta* continued. The men who followed Shannon as editor upheld the Union during the Civil War.

In 1865 the *Visalia Times* began publication and Visalia had a morning and evening paper until the two merged as the *Visalia Times Delta* in 1928.

VISALIA'S FIRST PUBLIC SCHOOL

The first public school, called the Little White School, was remembered fondly by those who attended classes there. Organized on May 4, 1857, it was located on Block 18 which today is bounded by School, Oak, Locust and Encina streets.

The Little White School was a whitewashed board and batten

Visalia's first public school, the Little White Schoolhouse, was built in 1857 on Block 18. It was used until 1872 when a larger school was built. Today the site is bounded by Locust, Encina, Oak and School streets.

building with a sheet metal roof. The teacher had a desk, but the children sat on logs placed on the dirt floor. The parents soon replaced the logs with homemade desks and later they added to the building and put down a plank floor. The first teacher was Joseph D. Travis.

The building was replaced in 1872 by a commodious two-story building on the same site. The night of the dedication, Christmas Eve 1872, was one that few persons forgot. Visalia had its one and only lynching that night when James McCrory was hanged from the Court Street bridge. Most of the school patrons had to walk over that bridge on the way home!

In 1890 the overcrowded school was replaced with a larger two-story building. It cost $30,000 and was named Tipton Lindsey School for a prominent Visalia attorney and state senator. That school was large enough to house both the grammar and high school students until a separate high school was built in 1897.

In 1920 the Tipton Lindsey School was torn down. The square became a city park until the Visalia City Library was built there in 1936. In 1976 the City of Visalia and the County of Tulare built the Visalia City-Tulare County Library on the same block under a joint powers agreement.

The site has two markers. In 1952 the Visalia Centennial Committee and the Visalia Charter Oak Parlor, Native Daughters of the Golden West, Number 272, dedicated a sidewalk marker to the memory of the pioneers who attended school there.

As part of the requirement for his Eagle Scout badge, Byron Jeske designed another plaque to commemorate the Little White School. It was placed on the west side of the library complex November 16, 1976.

> SITE OF VISALIA'S FIRST SCHOOL
> CALLED THE
> LITTLE WHITE SCHOOL
>
> BUILT IN MAY OF 1857
> JOHN D. TRAVIS WAS THE TEACHER
> THE SCHOOL STOOD UNTIL 1920
> WHEN IT WAS REPLACED BY AN
> EDUCATION INSTITUTION KNOWN AS
> VISALIA CITY LIBRARY

> SITE OF VISALIA'S FIRST SCHOOL
> CALLED THE
> "LITTLE WHITE SCHOOL"
> BUILT IN MAY OF 1857
> JOSEPH D. TRAVIS WAS THE TEACHER
> THE SCHOOL STOOD UNTIL 1920
> WHEN IT WAS REPLACED BY AN
> EDUCATIONAL INSTITUTION KNOWN AS
> VISALIA CITY LIBRARY

VISALIA'S FIRST SECONDARY SCHOOLS

Visalia's first high school was located in what is now Lincoln Oval in the north section of town. Built in 1897, it was used until 1911.

The first secondary schools in Visalia started within a few months of each other. The Visalia Select Seminary was organized as a joint stock company in 1860. The Academy of the Nativity was started in 1861 by Father Daniel Dade.

John Keener donated the land for the seminary. Today this land would be included in the grounds of the Kaweah District Delta Hospital. Thirty thousand dollars was subscribed in order to construct the two-story, eighty- by forty-foot building. The Reverend and Mrs. B. W. Taylor taught classes, while Mr. Taylor also served as pastor of the Methodist Episcopal Church South. The school provided for both day and boarding students, charging eight dollars a week for room and board. The students provided everything but food. The curriculum included the usual secondary subjects as well as art and handicrafts.

The building was damaged in the floods of 1862 and 1868. Money became a problem, and the school closed its doors. However, it was used for overflow classes from the public school until the new public school was built in 1872. The building deteriorated and until it was razed in the late 1870s had the reputation of being haunted.

Father Daniel F. Dade served as pastor of Saint Mary's Church in Visalia from 1861 to 1872. In 1861 he organized the Academy of the Nativity where he taught for the next ten years. It was located on Church Street between Race and Murray.

The Academy of the Nativity was started by Father Daniel Dade, beloved "Apostle of the Valley." The list of his students reads like a who's who of pioneer families, for children of all faiths attended Father Dade's school.

The academy took its name from the lower valley's first parish, the Church of the Nativity of the Blessed Virgin Mary, organized in the spring of 1861 by Father Dade. The name was appropriate because the only building he could find for the church was a brick stable. Father Dade remodeled the barn to include both the church and the school.

According to the prospectus, the course of instruction embraced all of the branches of a thorough English and commercial education together with the Latin, Greek, French, Spanish and Italian languages.

Father Dade's parish extended from Millerton to Havilah. In

order to cover that territory, the seemingly tireless priest rode three missionary circuits besides acting as pastor of Saint Mary's and teaching classes.

The school did not stay a strictly secondary school. Younger children enrolled and Father Dade had to hire a lay teacher for the primary department. It should also be noted that the men of Visalia asked Father Dade to teach night classes in bookkeeping, surveying and languages.

Father Dade's health became a matter of concern, and he left in 1872 to recuperate at Rhonerville in northern California. He died there a few months later. The academy struggled along for a time but without his leadership it was not practical to keep it open.

VISALIA'S FIRST STORE

In 1853 Nathan Baker built the first general store on what is now the southeast corner of Main and Bridge streets. In order to go from the fort to the store it was necessary to cross Mill Creek. A log bridge made the crossing possible and also gave Visalia its first named street, Bridge Street.

Ox teams brought supplies from Stockton. At a rate of sixty dollars a ton for freight, food and clothing came in barrels, bolts, kegs, boxes and tin-lined crates. Ready-made clothing was expensive and scarce. Shoes came unboxed. Old-timers recall with a certain nostalgia the delectable odors of a general store: a mingling of freshly ground coffee, salt mackerel, codfish and kerosene. Staple foods were scooped or picked out of uncovered containers, and somewhere on the counter lay the inevitable piece of jack cheese.

Merchants received payment when people sold cattle or grain, which meant the storekeeper operated on credit and faith in his fellow men. Pioneer women never had much money and often traded eggs or homemade butter for staples.

In 1857 Solomom Sweet bought Baker's store and Nathan Baker moved to Porterville, where he established another pioneer general store.

Historic Sites in the Northeast Portion of Tulare County

CENOTAPH

This oblisk in Memorial Park at Main and Park streets was originally in a small triangular park at the intersection of Main Street and Mooney Boulevard. It is a memorial to Visalia's war dead.

The Visalia American Legion Auxiliary #18 placed and dedicated the oblisk on May 30, 1929 as part of the Memorial Day observance. The parade that day included Spanish American War veterans, World War I veterans and five veterans from the Civil War. Color guards, fraternal organizations, and members of Company D, 185th Infantry made up the colorful parade.

The war to end all wars did not accomplish that goal, and since 1929 the American Legion Auxiliary has placed a commemorative plaque on the oblisk for those who died in World War II, the Korean War and in Viet Nam.

In 1982 the original site disappeared in the realignment of Highway 198 and Mooney Boulevard. The cenotaph was taken to a new park, Memorial Park, where it stands in a beautifully landscaped area.

CENTENNIAL TREE

There are several so-called centennial trees in Tulare County but only one was exhibited at the Centennial Exposition in Philadelphia in 1876. That tree grew about one hundred fifty feet northwest of General Grant Tree, and when it was felled in 1875 it was estimated to have been at least two thousand years old when Christ was born.

The destruction of the tree was pure commercial speculation. Many valley residents called it vandalism. Two brothers, William and Thomas Vivian, contracted to have the tree cut. It took the crew nine days to cut through the trunk sixteen feet above the ground. The mutilated stump measured twenty-eight feet four inches across.

The Centennial Tree, exhibited at Philadelphia in 1876.

The sixteen-foot section that was to be exhibited was hollowed out and cut into vertical sections which were hauled to Cross Creek and shipped by rail to Philadelphia. There the sections were carelessly cemented together. The exhibit was a failure since viewers could see the cemented joints and believed no tree ever grew that big.

The Centennial Tree was thought to be three hundred feet tall. Aside from the sixteen-foot exhibit section, a sixty-foot section was cut into fence posts. The rest of the splintered tree, the chips, and the foliage were piled on the stump and burned.

The Vivian brothers did not have permission to cut the tree, which was on federal land. They paid a fine but escaped a jail sentence which many people felt they deserved.

The Cenotaph was first located at the intersection of West Main Street and Mooney Boulevard in Visalia. It has been moved to Memorial Park at West Main and Hall streets.

This drawing of the red brick courthouse built in 1857 was done from a description furnished by Mrs. Mary McEwen, who was born in 1856 and lived to be 106 years old. The building was located on Block 21, bounded by Court, Church, Oak and Center streets.

COURT HOUSES OF TULARE COUNTY

The legislative act which created Tulare County on April 20, 1852 named Woodsville as the county seat and designated the Woods cabin as the courthouse. That cabin was built by men who had been led into the Four Creeks area in 1850 by John Woods. They started to clear the land and laid the foundations for five cabins, but only the Woods cabin was finished. Unwittingly, they had become involved in the general uprising of valley Indians that led to the Mariposa Indian War of 1851-52. In a running gun fight with the Indians on December 13, 1850, most of the men, including John Woods, were killed.

The Woods cabin served as the courthouse until September 1853 when the people voted to move the county seat from Woodsville to Visalia. Block Twenty-one in Visalia had been set aside for public buildings, but the new county had no building fund so a house on the northwest corner of Bridge and Oak streets, rented for seventy-five dollars a year, became the county's second courthouse.

On August 10, 1857, the board of supervisors let a contract to W. G. Russell to build a courthouse on Block Twenty-one. His bid was $1,000 and the county paid $400 in cash and the rest in county script. The building was inadequate for county purposes so the next year Redd, Palmer and Company were hired to build a new courthouse (number four) on the same site. It was a plain square red brick building. It faced west, giving students in the Little White School House a day-to-day view of local government. The upper story served as a courtroom and as the community center. In a burst of pride, the editor of the *Visalia Weekly Delta* noted that "the upper story was commodious enough to hold 1,000 people."

The lower floor had six jail cells lined with boiler plate. A gallows stood behind the courthouse since at that time county sheriffs were required to carry out death sentences.

In 1872 the tracks of the Southern Pacific Railroad reached the railroad's newly created town called Tulare. The plat map showed a square labeled "County Buildings." Between 1872 and 1876 there was open squabbling between Visalia and Tulare;

This courthouse was built in 1876 and used until 1957. Wings were added to the east and west in 1907, after this picture was taken.

Tulareans wanted to move the seat of justice to their city. Much to the consternation of the people in Tulare, in 1876 the state legislature authorized bonds for a new courthouse to be built on Block Twenty-one in Visalia.

A. A. Bennett, the architect of courthouse number five used the same plan that had been used for other California courthouses. The total cost of this building was approximately eighty thousand dollars, which included furnishings, landscaping and ornamentation. The cornerstone was laid October 27, 1876 amid ceremony and celebrities. That cornerstone is now on exhibit in courthouse number six.

Two wings were added to courthouse number five in 1907, and in 1934 a five-story west side addition was built.

By 1941 it was evident that more room was needed to take care of expanding county business. The supervisors set up a Court House Additional Building Fund financed by a special tax. Discussion reminiscent of that in 1876 began between those who wanted a new site for county buildings and those who wanted to build on Blocks Twenty-one and Twenty-two. The decision was hastened by the 1952 earthquake, which damaged the courthouse, and a site on West Main Extension and Mooney Boulevard was finally selected. The 1876 portion of the old courthouse was torn down but the 1934 addition was retained.

Courthouse number six was dedicated in December 1957, 100 years after courthouse number three was built on Block Twenty-one.

CUTLER PARK

Cutler Park was named for Dr. John Cutler (1819-1902), a venerated pioneer. He came to Tulare County from El Dorado County in 1852 and lived for a time in Fort Visalia. Dr. Cutler took up land east of Visalia in the Elbow Creek district. In 1859 he married Mrs. Nancy Rice Reynolds, widow of James Reynolds.

There is no record that he practiced medicine, although he enlisted as a surgeon during the Tule River War of 1856. He was always active in civic and community affairs. He represented El Dorado County in the third session of the state legislature and in

Cutler Park.

1853 served as judge of Tulare County. He also served an appointive term as superintendent of county schools and was a trustee of the Elbow Grammar School for many years.

When the Santa Fe Railroad came through the valley in 1897, Dr. Cutler deeded a right of way through his property and the railroad named the new community Cutler.

In 1919 his son, John Cutler, Jr., donated seventy-six acres of the home ranch as a memorial park for his parents. Cutler Park has many oak trees and the Saint John's River flows through it, making it a beautiful spot for picnickers.

ELECTION TREE AND WOODSVILLE

John Woods came to California in 1849 and traveled through the valley to the northern mines. In the fall of 1850 he came back

Election Tree, often called Charter Oak, is located east of Road 168 on Charter Oak Drive, about eight and a half miles east of Visalia.

to the delta of the Kaweah River as the leader of fourteen men who started to clear land for farming. They laid foundations for five cabins but only one was finished.

In 1850 the Yokuts were preparing to attack white settlers and miners who were taking over their lands. The first raid was made on Jim Savage's Fresno River trading post. The second attack came December 13, 1850. Chief Francisco had given Woods and his men ten days to leave, but they had made little attempt to comply and were in the field when the attack came. One man escaped after being wounded, and the rest were killed. Woods was the last to die, as he had run into the cabin when the attack began. From there he held off the Indians until his ammunition was gone. The Indians then rushed into the cabin, pulled him outside and killed him.

The legislative act which created Tulare County on April 20, 1852 named Woodsville (the small village growing up near the cabin) as the seat of justice and the cabin as the courthouse.

The organizational election for Tulare County was set for July 10, 1852. Most of the 109 voters came down from Mariposa County. Fifty-eight voted at Grand Island in Kings River and fifty-one came to Woodsville to vote in the cabin. The day was so hot the inspector moved the polling place from the cabin to the shade of an oak tree on the south side of the river which came to be called Election Tree.

In 1853 the people of Tulare County voted to move the seat of justice from Woodsville to Visalia. The next year Abraham Hilliard moved his family into the Woods cabin where they lived until their own house was completed. The cabin was razed in 1855 and the Goad family built a brick house on the site.

Woodsville was a busy place. The Stockton-Los Angeles road crossed the river at Woodsville. Stages, wagons, stock and footmen used the bridge which had replaced Dr. Payne's toll bridge.

In 1905 some men who had voted in the 1852 election were taken to that area. Almost six decades had passed since they had voted at Election Tree. The flood of 1862 had created Saint John's River and many oak trees had been cut. When the men were asked to point out Election Tree, they indicated a vigorous oak on the north side of the river about a mile from the obliterated site of Woodsville. History has not suffered from their understandable mistake!

In 1905 a wooden sign was placed on the designated tree. In 1949 the California Centennial Commission and the Tulare County Historical Society replaced the wooden sign with State Registered Landmark Number 410, using the same wording:

> UNDER THIS TREE A PARTY COMMANDED BY MAJOR JAMES D. SAVAGE, ON JULY 10, 1852, CONDUCTED AN ELECTION BY WHICH TULARE COUNTY WAS ORGANIZED. WOODSVILLE, SITE OF WOOD'S CABIN, THE FIRST SMALL TOWN SETTLED BY WHITE MEN IN TULARE COUNTY, AND FIRST COUNTY SEAT, WAS LOCATED ABOUT ONE-HALF MILE SOUTH OF THIS MARKER. THIS GENERAL AREA, THE DELTA OF THE KAWEAH RIVER, WAS ALSO KNOWN AS THE "FOUR CREEKS COUNTRY."

GENERAL GRANT TREE

Mrs. Lucretia Baker of Visalia was a member of a group which camped near a towering redwood in August 1867. She admired General Ulysses Grant and decided to write to him telling him that she had named the tree in his honor. This was his reply to her letter:

> Headquarters
> Armies of the United States
> Washington D.C.
> October 4, 1867
>
> My Dear Madam:
>
> Your favor of the 5th of September by express, accompanying a box containing branches, etc., from the largest tree in California, and no doubt in the world, which too partial friends have done me the honor to name after me is at hand. Please accept my thanks for thus remembering me and also for the kind expression of regard contained in your letter.
>
> With great respect,
> Your Obt. Svt., U. S. Grant, General
>
> To Mrs. Lucretia Baker
> Visalia, Tulare Co., Calif.

General Grant Tree.

Sequoia National Park was created September 25, 1890. Much to the surprise of local conservationists, General Grant National Park was created October 1, 1890. The reason remained a mystery for many years, but the intent at the time was to save a four-acre stand of very large redwood trees. The original grove had contained an estimated thirty-five hundred redwood trees in a 2,000-acre area before it was invaded by lumbermen. In 1890 the General Grant Tree, 264 feet in height with a base diameter of thirty-five feet, was the largest tree still standing in the grove.

On April 28, 1926, the General Grant Tree was dedicated as the nation's Christmas tree. On March 29, 1956, a joint resolution of Congress designated the world famous tree as a national shrine. Hundreds of people make a pilgrimage each Christmas to hold holiday services by the tree.

THE CHICAGO TREE
(GENERAL NOBLE TREE)

The most pretentious tree exhibit was sent to the Chicago World Columbian Exposition in 1893. By that time easteners had visited California and had seen or read about the big trees, so the exhibit was not regarded as a hoax, as earlier ones had been. The exhibit was sponsored by the United States Department of the Interior, which paid contractors $15,000 to prepare and deliver the section to be exhibited.

The selected tree, General Noble, grew three miles northwest of the entrance to General Grant National Park. It was cut fifty feet above the ground. The section to be prepared was cut into fourteen-foot staves hollowed out in the usual manner, crated and shipped to Chicago.

After the fair closed the tree sections were reassembled in a mall in Washington, D.C. and were an attraction for years. The sections were later stored at the Arlington Experimental Farm, where there is no record of them after 1942; so it is assumed they were discarded.

General Noble Tree, located in Converse Basin, was estimated to have been 3,196 years old when it was cut. Its stump is called Chicago Stump.

GENERAL SHERMAN TREE

This tree is regarded as the oldest and largest living thing on earth. The trunk and limbs of this giant redwood are scarred by the vicissitudes of the centuries of its existence.

General Sherman Tree.

The tree was discovered August 7, 1879 by James Wolverton, a hunter and trapper. He named it for General William Tecumseh Sherman, his commanding officer in the Civil War.

The age of the tree can only be estimated. Those who have made a study of tree rings believe it is over five thousand years old. During those millennia the tree was ravaged by fires which burned away large sections. The recuperative power of a sequoia is such that this giant has slowly healed itself. Naturalist Walter Fry began a study of the tree in 1902 and he estimated that by the year 2012 the wounds at the base would be entirely healed.

It is difficult to comprehend the size of the tree. Some figures may help. The estimated weight of the tree is 6,167 tons. If the trunk were cut into lumber, there would be enough to fill 280 railroad cars, at 40,000 pounds per car. Its height above mean base, 280 feet; base circumference, 102.7 feet; diameter 100 feet above the ground, 18.7 feet; height of largest branch, 130 feet; diameter of largest branch, 7.3 feet.

BEN HARRIS

Ben Harris (?-1933) has become part of the lore of the Sierra Nevada. No one who met him ever forgot him. His improbable, impossible yarns made him many friends and gained him the title of "The Greatest Liar in the Sierra Nevada."

He was orphaned as a young boy and was reared by the J. M. Hambright family, who had ranches near Farmersville and Lemon Grove. He did not finish school, for his real interest was

The Ben Harris marker is located at the Lemon Cove fire station.

the free life of a mountaineer. He worked for a lumber company and in the summer he guided people into the high mountain areas. He fished, hunted, prospected, and in his later years had a few horses to rent to campers.

Ben Harris died in 1933 and is buried in Visalia. No one knew his age. When asked, a friend pointed to the Sierra Nevada and said, "You see those mountains? Well, Ben was one year older than they are."

A marker for Ben Harris is placed in Lemon Cove.

BEN HARRIS

BEN HARRIS, UNWASHED AND PROFANE, WAS KNOWN AS THE GREATEST LIAR IN THE SIERRA. HE FREQUENTED LEMON COVE AND THE MINERAL KING BACK COUNTRY AND BECAME PART OF THE FOLK LORE.

HIS MULE WAS THE SMARTEST. HIS DOG THE MEANEST. HIS GUN THE SHOOTINGEST AND HIS EYE THE KEENEST FOR NIGH ON 75 YEARS. HE SHOULD BE REMEMBERED WHEN TALL TALES BRIGHTEN THE CAMP FIRE.

DR. SAMUEL GREGG GEORGE CHAPTER 1855
E C V
SEPT. 18, 1976

HOCKETT TRAIL

This historic trail took its name from John B. Hockett (1827-1898), who came overland to California in 1849 and camped on the Tule River on his way to the northern mines. He mined and freighted around Mariposa until he came to Visalia in 1859 to establish a general store. Five years later he moved his family to Porterville, where he was to be a major figure in the development of that community.

The Tulare County Board of Supervisors issued a franchise December 11, 1862 to Henry Cowden, Lyman Martin and John B. Hockett "to build a pack trail at a point in the Tulare Valley near where the Kaweah River leaves the foothills and thence easterly across the Sierras to the foot of Big Owens Lake between Haiwee Meadows and Lone Pine."

On August 5, 1864, Cowden presented a sworn statement that the three men had finished the trail at a cost of $1,000 and asked permission to charge tolls. The supervisors set the tolls at: mule or horse, fifty cents each; head of cattle, twenty-five cents each; sheep or hogs, five cents each; man on foot, twenty-five cents each.

The Hockett Trail was well marked and shortened the earlier Jordan Trail. One of the first persons to use the Hockett Trail was Clarence King, who in 1864 followed it on his way to climb Mount Whitney.

HOG WALLOWS

Large sections of the San Joaquin Valley were covered with mounds called hog wallows. They were fairly regular in shape, the largest being about fifty feet long, twenty feet wide and six feet high. In wet weather water accumulated at the base and dense clumps of tules grew in the marshy soil.

Hog wallows impeded travel. Old-timers said that riding over them in a stagecoach could only be compared to riding a bronco or sailing in a small boat in a storm. Large scale farming made it imperative to level the hog wallows.

Various theories have been proposed to explain the formation of the mounds. One suggested that patches of tules held soil washed down from the mountains. Another theory offered earthquakes as the causitive factor. Nearly all hog wallows had an underlay of hardpan so some thought that gas or water pressure coming up through the cracks had formed the mounds. Others said giant prehistoric gophers made the mounds. They were not far from the truth. The present scientific explanation (although some still dispute it) is that the mounds are made by the ordinary pocket gopher which is found working in the mima mounds in many parts of the country.

The Yokuts version may not be scientific, but it is as reasonable as some of the others. Their mythological hero, the eagle, created bird and animal people, but the coyote was such a nuisance that Eagle wanted to get away from him. Eagle told his people to build a high place where he could fly. They filled their work

A portion of the Hogwallow Preserve near Lindcove, off Avenue 314 near Road 220.

baskets, went eastward and piled the dirt higher and higher. When snow fell on their work, Eagle said it was high enough. He told them to go back down to the plains and dump what dirt was in their baskets. The high place is the Sierra Nevada and the hog wallows are the piles of dirt left by Eagle's people.

The Tulare County Historical Society as well as interested individuals sought to preserve a few acres of these dwindling mounds. In 1979 that effort was realized through the generosity of the Buckman family of Exeter. The inscription on the marker tells the story.

The Hogwallow Preserve marker is located at the site, Avenue 314 about one-eighth mile west of Road 220.

HOG WALLOW PRESERVE

THROUGH THE GENEROSITY OF CAROL BUCKMAN AND HER FATHER, PHILLIP E. BUCKMAN, M.D., THIS TEN ACRES OF PRIMITIVE LAND, NEVER CULTIVATED, HAS BEEN DONATED TO THE TULARE COUNTY HISTORICAL SOCIETY FOR PRESERVATION IN ITS NATURAL STATE IN PERPETUITY. THE ROUGH, MOUNDED LAND IS TYPICAL OF WHAT MUCH OF THE TULARE COUNTY PRAIRIE ALONG THE BASE OF THE SIERRA LOOKED LIKE BEFORE FARMING BEGAN. THE BUCKMANS, MEMBERS OF THE PIONEER FAMILY OF THAT NAME, HAVE SHARED WITH THE COUNTY HISTORIANS THE NEED TO PRESERVE AN EXAMPLE OF THESE PECULIAR STRUCTURES THE PIONEERS CALLED HOG WALLOWS.

TULARE COUNTY HISTORICAL SOCIETY
APRIL 22, 1979

HOSPITAL ROCK

Six miles above Sequoia National Park headquarters at Ash Mountain is a natural landmark known as Hospital Rock. This glacially split boulder is sixty feet long and twenty feet thick. It is split in such a way that the resultant sheltered circular room can accommodate twenty or more people comfortably.

In modern history several thousand Potwisha Indians lived nearby and the rock room was their tribal headquarters. It was also a place where sick Indians could recuperate. The location was ideal. There are still six species of acorn-bearing oak trees, and deer and small animals are plentiful even now. There are seed-bearing grasses and wild berries, and in the Kaweah River below Hospital Rock, fish are easy to catch.

The first white man in the area was Hale Tharp, who came to live in what is now Three Rivers in 1856. He was kind to the Indians who came to his Horse Creek ranch and they invited him to visit their mountain rancheria. Tharp needed a summer range for his stock so in the summer of 1858 he accepted Chief Chappo's invitation. Most of the Indians at the rancheria had never seen a white man and Tharp's horse, his clothes and equipment were subjects of good natured curiosity. Tharp said it was the cleanest camp he had ever been in. There were several sick people at the rock headquarters and although fires were kept burning there

Hospital Rock is six miles above Ash Mountain headquarters, Sequoia National Park.

were no smoke stains on the ceiling. Those are the contribution of white men.

The south side of the rock has a smooth surface covered with fading pictographs. The Indians begged Tharp to read the signs, for no one within their memory had been able to interpret them. Their folklore related that someday a man would come who could read the signs. Naturally, Tharp could not interpret the pictographs, for their message was in the mind of the one who drew them. It is evident from recent archaelogical work that Indians lived in that area many hundreds of years before the Potwishas came.

Tharp took up a summer range for his stock and made his camp inside a fallen hollow redwood. The date of his arrival, 1858, is carved in the bark and the tree is known to visitors in Sequoia National Park as Tharp's Log.

Hale Tharp spent every summer in the tree house from 1858 until 1890. As the first white visitor, he is credited as the discoverer of what is now Sequoia National Park and Giant Forest. He also named Hospital Rock because of care given there by the Indians to two white men who had suffered accidents.

Tharp took his stepson, John Swanson, to the summer range in 1860. The boy hurt his leg and Tharp took him to the tribal headquarters where the Indians applied a poltice of bear fat and jimson weed which healed the wound in a few days.

In 1873 Alfred Everton and George Cahoon set up gun traps for bears. Everton accidentally tripped a trap and was shot. Cahoon took him to the tribal rock where the Indians cared for him until he could be moved to Visalia.

Today Hospital Rock is visited by thousands of people on their way to Sequoia National Park. The park service maintains a small but comprehensive museum that offers a pictorial description of Indian life there long ago.

THOMAS JACOB

Thomas Jacob was an experienced nurseryman when he moved from San Jose to Tulare County in the early 1880s. He and his brother, Morphew Jacob, bought property in the Venice Hills district east of Visalia. They planted prunes, peaches, prunis simoni apricots, and citrus trees. They also set up a test station where tests of new fruit varieties were conducted for the state and for commercial nurseries. The ranch was a place of beauty with its driveways lined with palms, shrubs and colorful flowers.

For many years the Jacob brothers operated a nursery on Visalia's Main Street just west of the Holt Block. Their advertisements referred to the brothers as the "Kaweah Growers."

Walnut growers are agreed that the credit for introducing walnut culture into Tulare County must go to the Jacob brothers. In 1890 they planted a border of walnuts around 160 acres and demonstrated the commercial value of that crop.

Along with his many contributions to scientific agriculture, Thomas Jacob will be remembered for his role in the development of Mooney Grove Park. In 1910 he was appointed to the first Tulare County Board of Forestry whose immediate duty was to draw up a master plan for park development. It was at Mr.

The Jacob Brothers marker is placed on a rock containing a pestle and several mortar holes, found on the Jacob Ranch on Avenue 312.

Jacob's instigation that the board of supervisors put in bids for the two famous statues, "The End of the Trail" and "The Pioneer."

In 1978 the Dr. Samuel G. George Chapter of E Clampus Vitus dedicated a plaque to the Jacob brothers. It is on the Jacob ranch.

THOMAS JACOB   MORPHEW JACOB
1852-1930   1862-1925

FOUNDERS OF THE SAN JOAQUIN VALLEY WALNUT DISTRICT

E CLAMPUS VITUS
DSGG 1855
DEDICATED OCTOBER 28, 1978

LONE OAK CEMETERY

Lone Oak Cemetery is the oldest public cemetery in the lower Valley. Its name came from a lone oak tree which was shattered by lightning many years ago. The present fenced-in cemetery is but a pitifully small part of the original cemetery.

Lone Oak is near Woodsville and it is reasonable to think that the first burials were the members of the Woods party killed in 1850. A trip to the site of Woodsville substantiates this, for the soldiers who came from Fort Miller after the raid would not have buried the victims by the river.

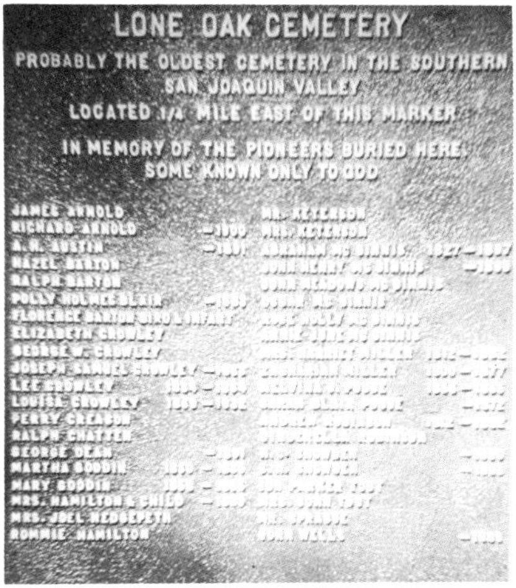

The Lone Oak Cemetery marker is on Road 168 near Avenue 324.

The Visalia Cemetery was used first in 1854 and Deep Creek in 1859, and there were almost certainly burials in Lone Oak earlier than the first recorded one, that of James Crowley in 1863.

As time passed so did the wooden headboards. Vandals destroyed most of the marble stones; so individual burial places cannot be located.

Citrus orchards and grain fields began to encroach on the unfenced land until the original boundaries were obscured. In 1930 a group of people who had relatives buried in Lone Oak were given permission to fence in what was left of the cemetery.

The Kaweah Chapter, Daughters of the American Revolution and the Tulare County Historical Society dedicated a plaque listing all of the known burials.

LONE OAK CEMETERY

PROBABLY THE OLDEST CEMETERY IN THE SOUTHERN SAN JOAQUIN VALLEY. LOCATED ONE MILE EAST OF THIS MARKER.

IN MEMORY OF THE PIONEERS BURIED HERE—SOME KNOWN ONLY TO GOD.

ERECTED BY
TULARE COUNTY HISTORICAL SOCIETY
KAWEAH CHAPTER DAR
1970

MOONEY GROVE PARK

Mooney Grove Park is the best known landmark in Tulare County. It is also the last sizeable remnant of the great oak forest which once stretched from the foothills to the shore of Tulare Lake.

The recorded history of the park goes back to July 1806 when Father Jose Zalvidea and Lieutenant Francisco Ruiz left Santa Barbara seeking locations for a proposed inland mission chain. The tired, hot soldiers who were with them must have welcomed the shade of the oak forest. Father Zalvidea wrote that the arid plains were only fit to grow sunflowers, but that their camp had all the prerequisites for a mission: a small stream, timber, fertile soil, and most important, receptive Indians.

During the next decade other Spaniards visited the oak forest and recommended the location for a mission and a presidio. Unfortunately, the Mexican Revolution and the secularization of the missions stopped all plans for occupation of the Valle de los Tulares.

Benjamin Willis settled in what is now the park in 1852 and patented the land in 1860. In 1878 he sold the ranch to Michael Mooney. Mr. Mooney was a Visalia merchant and civic leader who bought the Willis ranch for a family home. He died in 1881 but the Mooney family continued to live on the ranch.

The long struggle to save the giant redwoods of the Sierra Nevada began in Visalia. After Sequoia and General Grant national parks were created in 1890, local conservationists realized that the valley oaks were disappearing.

Michael Mooney's son, Hugh Mooney, was one of the local conservationists. He had had attractive offers for the ranch, including an offer of $15,000 to cut the oak trees for firewood. Instead, Hugh Mooney offered the County of Tulare 100 acres of the ranch for $15,000. On August 9, 1909, the board of supervisors authorized the purchase of the land. The deed stipulated that the land should be maintained as a public park for the enjoyment of people, and that none of the trees should be cut unless they were in a diseased or dying condition.

A board of forestry was appointed to facilitate the development of the park. The original master plan included "roads, walks, necessary bridges, additional planting, and clearing of brush." Johannes Reimers from San Joaquin County was hired to develop the master plan.

In 1912 the pavilion, which is remembered with nostalgia, was built, and in 1913 George Anderson was hired as chief forester. Board member William Bartlett proposed the creation of a lagoon to beautify the park and to add boating to the recreational facilities. In 1916 a small zoo was added. Today, ducks, geese and peacocks roam the park, mingling with their wild cousins, begging shamelessly for handouts from picnickers.

Two large statues near the entrance gates are world famous. Both were exhibited at the Panama Pacific International Exposition in San Francisco in 1915. As are most fair statues, they were made of non-permanent materials. The Tulare County Board of Forestry put in a successful bid for Solon Borglum's "The Pioneer" when the exposition closed. The statue arrived in Visalia May 2, 1916 and was placed near the north gate of the park. It stood until May 28, 1980, when a strong earthquake shook the valley and the statue collapsed.

The Board of Forestry also bid on "The End of the Trail" by James Fraser. A San Francisco club had raised money to place it a bluff overlooking the bay but could not promise permanent care of the statue. Much to the surprise of the board of foresttry, "The End of the Trail" arrived in Visalia September 10, 1919. It was placed near the southern gate entrance.

In 1968 the Western Heritage Center and Cowboy Hall of Fame began to acquire working models for their James Earle

The entrance to the Tulare County Museum and pioneer village. This first building was dedicated in 1948 to the memory of Hugh Mooney.

Fraser Hall. "The End of the Trail" in the park was a working model. It was traded for a bronze replica which was mounted in a moat near the original setting. Since the statue was first exhibited in 1915 in San Francisco, it is said to be one of the most photographed statues in the country.

On April 25, 1948, the cornerstone of the Tulare County Museum in the park was dedicated to the memory of Hugh Mooney. Today the museum houses one of the finest collections of artifacts, farm machinery, Indian baskets, pictures, and buildings that may be found in California.

The historical significance of Mooney Grove Park is related on a marker near the north entrance.

This marker is located near the north entrance to Mooney Grove Park on Mooney Boulevard.

MOONEY GROVE

THIS PLAQUE IS DEDICATED TO THE MEMORY OF THOSE WHO PRESERVED THIS REMNANT OF THE FOREST OF VALLEY OAKS THAT FORMERLY COVERED THE KAWEAH DELTA.

VISITED BY FATHER ZALVIDEA IN 1806 WHILE SEARCHING FOR A MISSION SITE, THE AREA WAS A RENDEZVOUS FOR LATER EXPLORATIONS.

SETTLED BY BENJAMIN WELLS IN 1852, THIS LAND WAS PURCHASED BY MICHAEL MOONEY AND WAS OWNED BY THE MOONEY FAMILY UNTIL ACQUIRED FOR PARK PURPOSES BY TULARE COUNTY IN 1909.

TULARE COUNTY HISTORICAL SOCIETY
OCTOBER 26, 1958

KAWEAH POSTOFFICE

The Kaweah postoffice on the North Fork of the Kaweah River is a ten- by twelve-foot weather-beaten structure. The tiny porch has a bulletin board with the usual postoffice posters. The mail boxes are inside although the lobby can accommodate only two or three people at a time.

The building is important because of its association with the Kaweah Co-operative Colony. That pretentious socialistic group originated in San Francisco in 1885 and attracted members from all parts of the nation. The colony took its name from the river and its goals from dreams. After a few years of strife and struggle, the utopian dream collapsed. Nevertheless, the colonists made remarkable contributions to the history of Three Rivers and Tulare County. Using picks, shovels and grit, they built a road into what is now Sequoia National Park which was used until 1927. The colonists built and operated a sawmill. They printed a newspaper on the first steam press used in the county. They were decades ahead of their time in dealing with human rights. Men and women had equal pay and opportunities to work. They devised a monetary system based on the substitution of time for money.

The colony had several semi-permanent camps. One was Advance, which was granted a postoffice May 17, 1890. Henry Hubbard was the first postmaster. Later that year the name was

The first Kaweah postoffice was located at the colony's semi-permanent camp at Advance. The present postoffice and marker are located above Three Rivers on the North Fork Road.

changed to Kaweah and Fred Hirshady was appointed postmaster. From time to time the building was moved to meet the needs of its patrons, or to accommodate the postmaster. Mrs. Horace Taylor was the third postmaster, and later the office was in the home of Charles Keller. When he resigned John Weckert took over.

Many colonists stayed in the Three Rivers area after the colony disbanded. In 1910 the patrons furnished labor and materials for a new building. That structure is the present postoffice. Theodore Gross remained as postmaster until 1925. The next year Mrs. Ida Purdy was appointed postmaster and became firmly linked with Kaweah postoffice history. The Purdys had been members of the Kaweah Colony and although they left to teach in other parts of California, they loved Three Rivers and came back to their ranch. The postoffice was some distance from the Purdys' house so the patrons put the small building on logs and rolled it downhill. For the next twelve years Mrs. Purdy and Mrs. Viva May alternated in the position of postmaster.

Mrs. Purdy died in 1969. The Tulare County Historical Society used the memorial donations given in her name to commission an oil painting of the Kaweah postoffice which now hangs in the Tulare County Museum.

In 1948 State Registered Landmark Number 389 was placed near the Kaweah postoffice. A first day cover was designed for stamp collectors and 5,000 cachets were mailed from the postoffice to collectors all over the nation.

KAWEAH POSTOFFICE

THE KAWEAH COOPERATIVE COLONY WAS A UTOPIAN PROJECT STARTED IN 1886. FOR SEVERAL YEARS IT ATTRACTED INTERNATIONAL ATTENTION AND MANY SETTLERS CAME HERE AND ACTUALLY DID MUCH TO FURTHER THEIR IDEALS. UNABLE TO SECURE TITLE TO THE LAND AND BECAUSE OF INTERNAL DIFFICULTIES THE ORGANIZATION CEASED TO EXIST AFTER 1892, LEAVING AS ONE OF ITS TANGIBLE REMINDERS THE KAWEAH POSTOFFICE.

MARKER PLACED BY THE CALIFORNIA CENTENNIALS COMMISSION. BASE FURNISHED BY THE TULARE COUNTY HISTORICAL SOCIETY.

OCTOBER 24, 1948

MARK TWAIN TREE

In 1891 Collis Huntington arranged to donate a specimen of a big tree to the American Museum of Natural History in New York City and another to the British Museum in London. The selected tree, the Mark Twain, was near the entrance to Kings Canyon National Park. It had been saved from earlier logging operations because it was too big for the sawmill equipment of that era. When it was cut in 1891, the ring count showed its age to be 1,314 years. The cut was made twelve feet above the ground where the base measured sixteen and a half feet in diameter.

Mark Twain Tree.

The cut section was sawed into slabs and shipped from Monson on flat cars. The exhibit in New York drew huge crowds of people who were fascinated by the size of the tree.

The rest of the Mark Twain Tree was cut into fence posts. The stump of the tree was leveled and used as a dance floor.

THE POGUE HOTEL

John William Center Pogue (1839-1907) came to California in 1857 in a wagon train led by the Reverend Jonathan Blair. He married Blair's daughter Nancy and in 1862 moved his family to Tulare County. Their first home was near Venice Hills. They later moved near Bravo Lake (Woodlake) but were washed out in the flood of 1868 and moved to Dry Creek. In 1877 Mr. Pogue began to experiment with citrus culture. He is credited with starting the successful citrus industry around what is now Woodlake and Lemon Cove.

Nora Pogue Montgomery stands beside the Pogue Hotel marker in Lemon Cove.

THE POGUE HOTEL

ON THIS SITE IN 1879, A LARGE TWO STORY THIRTEEN ROOM HOTEL WAS CONSTRUCTED, KNOWN AS "THE COTTONWOODS," BY THE PARTNERSHIP OF C. W. CROCKER AND J. B. WALLACE OF SAN FRANCISCO AND J. W. C. POGUE. THE POGUE FAMILY CAME TO THIS LIME KILN AREA IN 1865 AND EVENTUALLY OWNED OVER TEN THOUSAND ACRES. HERE, MR. POGUE PLANTED CITRUS IN 1877.

HE BECAME SOLE OWNER OF THE HOTEL AND PARTNERSHIP IN 1881 AND THIS WAS HIS HOME UNTIL HIS DEATH IN 1907. THE BUILDING REMAINED IN THE POGUE FAMILY UNTIL 1936 WHEN NORA POGUE MONTGOMERY, THE YOUNGEST OF THE NINE POGUE CHILDREN, WHO WAS BORN IN THIS HOUSE, GAVE IT TO THE LEMON COVE WOMAN'S CLUB. IT WAS REMODELLED TO BECOME A CLUBHOUSE AND COMMUNITY CENTER. IT WAS THE FIRST HOUSE IN THE LEMON COVE TOWNSITE LAID OUT BY MR. POGUE IN 1894.

TULARE COUNTY HISTORICAL SOCIETY
MAY 8, 1977

RANCHO DE KAWEAH

In 1888 the Lindsay Land Company bought several thousand acres of land around what would develop as the City of Lindsay. The land was subdivided and sold with water rights. With the exception of Lewis Creek there are no rivers in that area so the company planned to bring irrigation water from the Kaweah River.

Plans were underway to develop a well field when John J. Cairns, also from Lindsay, successfully demonstrated that water could be pumped from an underground water table. Pumped water quickly transformed dry fields into orchards of citrus, olives, grapes and decidious fruits. Over-planting and over-pumping, plus a series of dry years, depleted the water table and the original plan for a well field was revived by the Lindsay-Strathmore Irrigation District. That district, formed in 1915, bought 1,100 acres of land southwest of Woodlake and near the Kaweah River. The property, formerly the Hyde Ranch, was renamed Rancho de Kaweah, and thirty-nine wells were bored. Water was pumped through a low level canal to a main booster station north of Lindsay, through six miles of gravity bench flume on Elephant Hill to a second booster station and on to the El Mirador Reservoir. There were ninety miles of underground distribution mains.

In 1916 a group of irrigation districts, led by the Tulare Irrigation District, filed a suit against the Lindsay-Strathmore Irrigation District charging that the well field at Rancho de Kaweah was depleting their water supply. In substance this was the age-old conflict between riparian water rights and the right of appropriation. Riparian rights came from the common law of England and had been written into the constitution of California. The right of appropriation developed in western America where water rights were hotly contested.

Earl Vincent, left, and Kenneth Vincent at Rancho de Kaweah, on Road 196 north of Highway 198.

The case was emotionally draining, for no matter which side won, the farmers on the losing side faced disaster.

Before the lawsuit ended twenty years later, seven judges had heard testimony, 37,000 pages of transcript had piled up, and 600 exhibits had been submitted. Each reluctant decision was in favor of the plaintiffs and was appealed by the defendants. Finally, on December 17, 1936, Judge Irwin handed down a compromise decision that was accepted because the Central Valley Water Project was finished.

The visible part of Rancho de Kaweah remained until 1956. That was the ninety-foot "bubble tower tank." It was built in 1919, not to store water but as a pressure equalizer for the pipeline that carried water to the Lindsay-Strathmore Canal. The crew which took it down had hoped to salvage the lumber, but the heavy tank fell during the process and most of the lumber splintered.

SAN JOAQUIN ROLLING MILL

The forty acres on which this mill stood were patented in 1860 by Isaac Lewis who then deeded the land to Harvey Russell. The land in the area was known for years as "the swamp" because of ditch water there.

In 1865 John Nelson bought the forty acres for $100 and built a grist mill powered by a water wheel in the ditch. Nelson had borrowed $1,400 from Nathan Dillon and after the property was heavily damaged in the 1868 flood, he deeded the property plus two shares of ditch stock to Dillon.

Nathan Dillon (1820–1903) came to Tulare County in 1852. He was an astute and successful businessman who later became identified with the lumber industry east of Porterville. Dillonwood is named for him.

When Dillon took over the grist mill he called it the Illinois Mill and sold flour under that trade name. The mill also ground corn meal and later manufactured rolled barley and oats for stock feed. Dillon leased the mill for fifty dollars a month, giving the operator an option to buy if he would put in approximately twenty-five hundred dollars in improvements. In subsequent

The San Joaquin Roller Mill is east of Visalia on Highway 198, across from the fish hatchery.

The San Joaquin Roller Mill marker.

years the mill changed ownership several times with Dillon holding mortgages on the property. In 1881 the name was changed to Eagle Mill and a steam engine was added to operate the machinery when ditch water was low.

John Firebaugh, Exeter pioneer, bought the mill in 1888 and renamed it the San Joaquin Rolling Mill. A few years later it was burned and then rebuilt. In 1897 Firebaugh deeded the property back to Nathan Dillon, who had held the mortgage.

After Dillon's death in 1903, his heirs leased the property to August Bohnert and sold it to him in 1909. The Bohnert family operated the San Joaquin Rolling Mill until they sold it in 1914. The new owner dismantled the building.

Doctor Samuel G. George Chapter, E Clampus Vitus has placed a marker near the mill site.

SAN JOAQUIN ROLLING MILL

ONE OF THE FIRST FLOUR ROLLER MILLS IN CALIFORNIA, LOCATED JUST TO THE NORTH OF THE PEOPLE'S DITCH. THIS MILL, OPERATING FROM 1854 TO 1913, PRODUCED MUCH OF THE FLOUR USED BY THE EARLY SETTLERS OF THE VALLEY.

E CLAMPUS VITUS
DSGG 1855
DEDICATED OCTOBER 28, 1978

Part 3
Historic Sites in the Southeast Portion of Tulare County

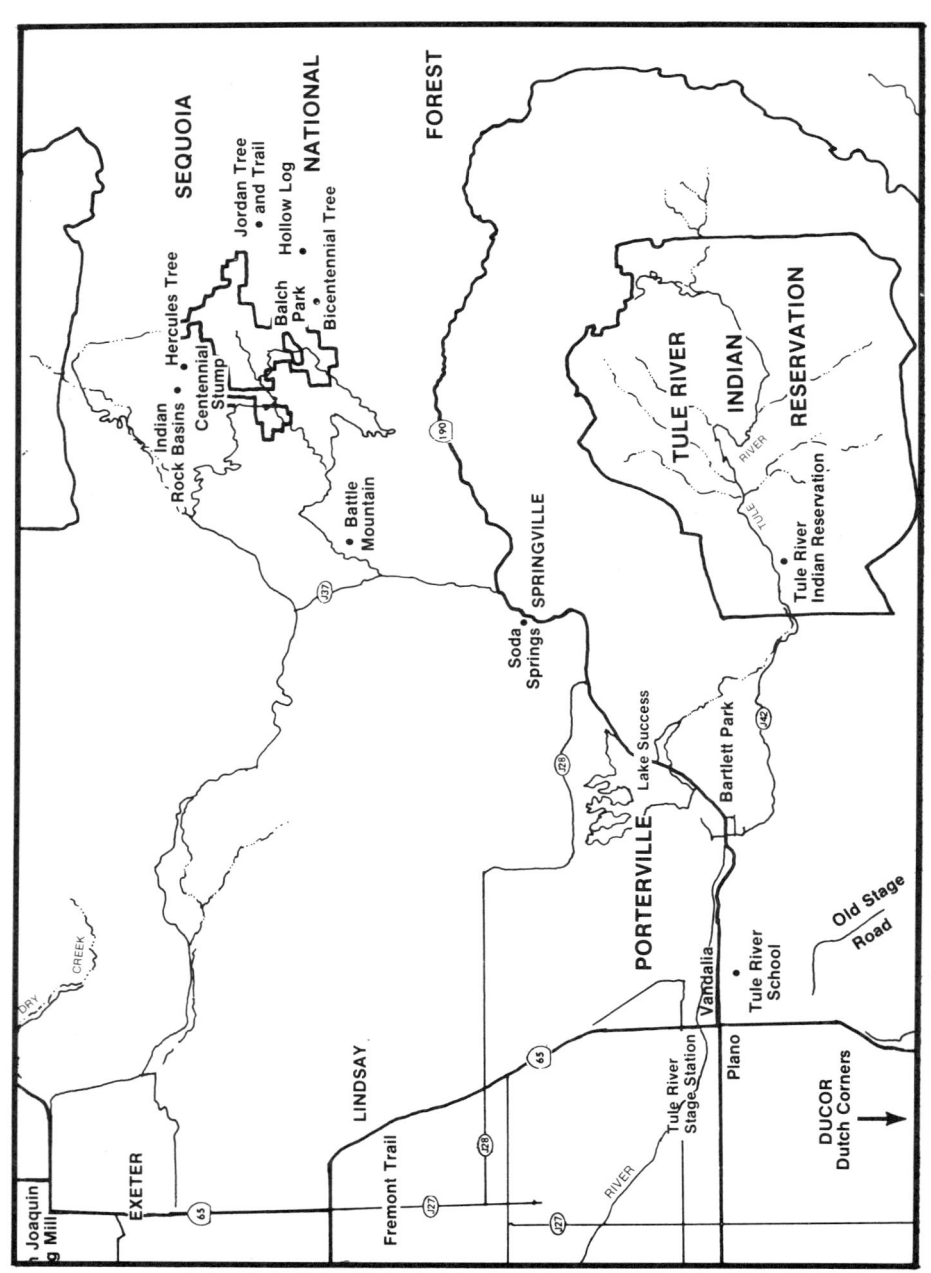

Historic Sites in the Southeast Portion of Tulare County

BALCH PARK

In 1885 John J. Doyle homesteaded Talbott Meadows thirty-four miles east of Porterville. Doyle had been one of the prominent participants in the Mussel Slough tragedy five years before and with four other men had been imprisoned for eight months.

Mr. Doyle loved the mountains and the big trees. He subdivided part of his homestead and sold 125 lots so others could have summer homes amid the pine and redwood trees. The resort became known as Summer Home. Nearby was Mountain Home, another summer resort, developed by the A. J. Doty family.

In 1905 John Doyle sold much of his property to the Mount Whitney Power and Electric Company, a Tulare County corporation. He was dismayed when he learned that the company planned to cut many of the big trees to build a flume. Mrs. John H. Hammond, one of the principal stockholders, was equally upset by the news and managed to have that project postponed.

In involved legal transactions the company was sold to the Southern California Edison Company. One of the officers in that company was A. C. Balch of Los Angeles, who was also an officer of the San Joaquin Light and Power Company, based in Fresno.

Mr. Doyle learned that Mr. Balch and his wife were interested in buying land to donate for public parks. He visited them and described the mountain resorts. They bought a tract and on October 2, 1923 offered the land to Tulare County, stipulating that the county build a road to the land. The road was finished in 1929 and on December 23, 1930 the Tulare County Board of Supervisors formally accepted the gift and officially named it Balch Park.

BARTLETT PARK

William Pitt Bartlett (1855-1929) either edited or published newspapers before he came to Porterville in 1901. During that time he was also involved in the manufacture of newsprint. One of the filler ingredients of newsprint was calcined magnesite,

The old location of Bartlett Park was east of Porterville on the Tule River.

and publishers were seeking new sources of that mineral.

Large deposits of magnesite had been discovered around Porterville as early as 1857, by Dr. S. G. George. Dr. George filed claims on the deposits but let the claims lapse.

Around the turn of the century the claims were "rediscovered" and developed by large corporations. Mr. Bartlett came to Porterville to manage one of them, the Willamette Pulp and Paper Company. He quickly became involved in community affairs and devoted considerable energy toward the conservation of natural resources. In 1907 he was named to the Porterville Park Commission, an appointment he held until his death. In 1910 he was named to the new Tulare County Board of Forestry, another lifelong appointment. That board drew up the master plan for the development of Mooney Grove Park and also planned the acquisition of the famous statues, "The Pioneer" and "The End of the Trail."

In 1923 the Porterville Chamber of Commerce sponsored a drive to buy land for a city park. The site selected was east of Porterville and adjacent to Tule River. The land was cleared of brush, a swimming hole was deepened and picnic tables were built. Much of the work was supervised by Mr. Bartlett. The park was first called Tule Park, but after a couple of years citizens successfully petitioned to have the name changed to Bartlett Park for the man who had done so much in the dual fields of conservation and preservation.

When Success Dam was built in 1955 Bartlett Park was submerged. A new site of 210 acres south of the old park was purchased and carries the name, Bartlett Park.

BATTLE MOUNTAIN

Although one must walk to find the location, a few stones are left to remind us of Tulare County's only Indian war.

The Mariposa Indian War of 1851-52 was supposed to have broken the original resistance of the Indians in the Mother Lode. By 1856 settlers and miners were coming into land adjacent to the Kaweah, Kings, Tule and Kern rivers and were driving the Indians from their land. Many of the miners were young and daring and did not like Indians. They were just waiting for an excuse to start a fight.

In March 1856 an unnamed cowboy rode into Visalia yelling that 500 head of cattle had been stolen by Indians. The men who investigated learned that one calf had been stolen from a man in Frazier Valley. Then, Orson K. Smith's sawmill just east of Visalia was burned, and again the Indians were blamed.

On March 18, Judge John Cutler authorized Dr. Samuel G. George to open a roll book for a company of mounted riflemen to be equipped and paid by the State of California. Fifty-six men signed up and elected Foster De Masters as captain. Messages were sent to the mining camps, and a second company was organized, with William G. Poindexter as captain. The muster roll shows a total of 132 names in the two companies.

A close-up of boulders piled up to make the fort at Battle Mountain.

The newly-assembled riflemen trailed the Indians up the north fork of the Tule River and found a surprise. The Indians were protected behind a strong fort. Colonel George Stewart later described it as "a line of breastworks, from 2 to 4 feet high, composed of boulders and brush, extending a distance of 80 yards along the face of a hill at the head of a little cove or plain. The ground in front was open and rough. In the rear of the fort was a dense growth of scrub brush and chaparral."

The muster roll shows that the fighting lasted from April 20 to May 16, 1856. The Indians were finally defeated when soldiers from Fort Miller arrived with a howitzer. Few white men were injured, but several Indians were killed, the exact number unknown because the Indians retreated into the surrounding brush. The white men fanned out into the mountains and burned all of the caches of food they could find.

The confrontation was sobering to the white men, for the Indians had been armed with bows and arrows and a very few guns. There was little doubt that the Indians could have run the white men out of the lower valley, had they had equal arms.

The most important aspect of the Tule River Indian War of 1856 was the establishment of the Tule River Indian Reservation in 1857.

BICENTENNIAL TREE

California, as were all of the states, was asked to select a tree to dedicate during the Bicentennial year. It was entirely fitting that the redwood was selected by the California Legislature. Many redwood trees were planted throughout the state during the year.

Bicentennial Tree.

The Bicentennial Tree marker is located in Balch Park.

In Tulare County a search was begun for a suitable sequoia gigantea. One in Balch Park estimated to be 1,800 years old was selected and was dedicated "as a silent sentinel through the ages, watching the parade of mankind and progress go by." The marker reads:

TULARE COUNTY BICENTENNIAL TREE
DEDICATED AUGUST 8, 1976
BY THE TULARE COUNTY
REVOLUTIONARY BICENTENNIAL COMMISSION

BOOT HILL

The only Boot Hill in the lower valley is in Tailholt fifteen miles southeast of Ducor. Tailholt was a prosperous mining and trading center that came into existence during the 1850s. When a postoffice was granted in 1862 the name was officially changed to White River.

Boot Hill should not be confused with the White River Cemetery on Bald Mountain. Boot Hill is located on a sloping hillside to the left of the road that enters the old camp. The graves are not marked but they may be located by indentations in the soil.

Five of the seven known occupants died violently. Two were buried under unusual circumstances.

Daniel Poer, the first occupant of Boot Hill, was shot December 20, 1862 by Matt Wells after he called Wells a Black Republican. Wells slipped out of Tailholt but was later exonerated by the inquest jury. He came back and a few years later served a term as sheriff of Kern County.

On the evening of April 8, 1863, Daniel Lane and Jerry Robinson quarreled over Civil War politics. Lane pulled a knife but Robinson was quicker with his gun. The inquest jury returned a verdict of self defense.

The third victim was also named Daniel. Daniel Daugherty tried to ride his horse into a saloon and was thrown out. He came back without his horse and started arguing about politics. How or by whom he was shot is a mystery, for so far no inquest record has been found.

The notorious Jack Gordon was killed December 15, 1864, by his partner, Samuel Groupie. Jack Gordon was an alias used by Peter Worthington, who had left an unsavory trail through old Mexico and the Apache country. In the early 1850s he ran stock at Tulare Lake and had his camp at Gordon's Point on the northwest shore. He also worked mining claims on Gordon's Gulch at White River. Undoubtedly Gordon was a member of the Mason-Henry Guerrila gang which operated in the valley during that era.

Gordon and Groupie shared a cabin in Tailholt but were not friendly. They divided their holdings, which included some hogs. Gordon butchered his hogs and hung them near the cabin. Some miners hid Groupie's hogs, put his ear marks on Gordon's hogs and waited for some fun when the men came back from their mines. Groupie came first and was furious. When Gordon came to the cabin the men exchanged a few angry words and before Gordon could pull his gun, Groupie shot him. Gordon died within a few hours. Groupie slipped out of camp and was never apprehended.

Jack Gordon had accumulated a modest fortune and if the last man to whom he talked did not find the cache, it is probably still buried in Gordon Gulch.

Boothill Cemetery is located in White River (Tailholt). It can be seen in this photograph on the slope of the hill in the right foreground. Several gravesites are visible. The house in the left corner was the dance hall. The building in the front center was the school built in 1876.

Thomas Jones and James Utley were also mining partners who constantly quarreled although they, too, lived in the same cabin and worked the same mine. On February 27, 1880 Jones was eating inside the cabin when Utley sneaked in and shot him in the back. Utley was gone by the time the body was found. He was held to answer by the inquest jury, but like Groupie, he was never located.

Two burials held under odd circumstances were those of Chescott, an Indian girl, and John Parker, who hated women.

Jack Gordon had found Chescott wandering alone and apparently lost. She was too young to tell him anything but her name. Gordon took her to Woody and paid a family to take care of her. After Gordon's death, Mr. and Mrs. Levi Mitchell, who lived in Tailholt, took care of Chescott. The girl died in her late teens and the community thought it fitting that she should be buried near Jack Gordon. Her grave is actually on the slope of the hill away from the other graves.

John Parker always said he hated women. As he lay dying in 1896 he asked his fellow miners to bury him on Boot Hill so he "would not have to rise up on resurrection day with women." His odd wish was carried out by his friends, who suspected he wanted to atone for something in his past life, but in 1896 Chescott's grave had been forgotten, so Parker's dying hope may not be fulfilled!

CENTENNIAL STUMP

Centennial Stump in Mountain Home State Forest is often confused with the real Centennial Tree. There was no reference to the "stump" when this tree was cut. That was understandable since it was cut shortly after the fiasco perpetrated by the Vivian brothers. (See page 31.) The men who cut this tree may have intended to exhibit it in 1876, but the most reliable information indicates that it was cut between 1877 and 1878.

The cut was made twenty-eight feet above the ground where the tree measured twenty-six feet in circumference. The tree was estimated to have been over three thousand years old.

The section for exhibition was cut into long slabs which were

Centennial Stump, located in Mountain Home State Forest.

hauled out of the mountains on roads made especially for the trip. For a short time the rejoined slabs were exhibited in Visalia. They were then dismantled, hauled to Tulare and shipped by railroad to San Francisco where they were exhibited in Woodward Gardens.

DUTCH CORNERS (DUCOR)

In 1885 four German men took up homesteads in T 23 R 27 S 34. One of the prerequisites for completing homestead ownership was a water well. Thrift and common sense led the men to sink a well where the four corners of their homesteads met, and that junction became Dutch Corners.

The plains around Dutch Corners were used as rangeland for sheep and cattle and for growing various grains. The men who had the courage to plant grain were called sky farmers because their crops depended entirely upon rainfall.

This marker is in front of the original general store in Dutch Corners, now the Dutch Frontier Restaurant on Avenue 56. The hose cart was bought by the community in 1910.

As the east side of the county began to attract settlers, the Southern Pacific Railroad built a line in the area, in 1888. Someone who dealt out railroad names decided to condense Dutch Corners into Ducor.

Railroads and deep well pumping changed land use patterns all over the southern valley. Land colonies were incorporated, usually by outsiders, and small farms were sold. The Ducor Land Company was formed in 1909 by local men who had local property interests: Shade Braly, Charles Tibbens, John Dennis, S. Richard Shoup and J. W. Righter.

Even before the land company was formed the nucleus of community life had started. Ducor had homes, a school, a church, a Rochdale store, a hotel and annex, a post office, a blacksmith shop, a livery stable and a grain warehouse. By 1914 there were several dry goods stores, a bakery, a meat market, a branch of the county library, a small community building housing a fire hose wagon, a two-story brick bank, a drug store, a lumber yard, a barley mill, a garage, a newspaper, a stock loading corral and a telephone company.

Like many small agriculturally based communities, Ducor never fulfilled its potential. Today it is surrounded by large grain farms, cattle ranges, citrus orchards and vineyards. Water from the Friant-Kern Canal has made possible the use of land once thought fit only for sky farming.

FIRST ORANGE TREES

Tulare County produces more citrus than any other county in California. Two women started the industry but since neither realized she was making history, the year will have to be guessed at as either 1862 or 1863.

Mrs. Huffman White lived in Frazier Valley near Porterville. The White family were visiting friends in Visalia and were invited to a July Fourth observance at Camp Babbitt. The soldiers gave the children oranges imported from the Sandwich Islands. Mrs. White saved the seeds and planted them at the White ranch. One tree matured and bore ten oranges which she sold for one

The first commercial orange grove was at 271 East Gibbon Street in Porterville, now owned by Mr. and Mrs. Rodney Homer.

dollar each. She gave the money to her church. That tree continued to bear fruit for more than half a century.

Mrs. Deming Gibbons, who lived in Plano, also visited in Visalia and her children were also given oranges by the soldiers. Mrs. Gibbons planted the seeds and two trees matured. Mr. Gibbons began to experiment with citrus and planted and replanted until he had a grove of seventy-four trees. His grove attracted state-wide attention when his fruit won first prize at the Los Angeles Citrus Fair in 1883. Until then it was assumed that the Tehachapi Mountains marked the northern climatic barrier for citrus.

L. W. Prestage bought the Gibbons ranch in 1899 and budded all but one row of oranges to the new Washington Navel. The property is now owned by his grandson, Rodney Homer. Several of the unbudded trees are still in vigorous condition in spite of their age.

DR. SAMUEL GREGG GEORGE

Dr. Samuel Gregg George (1814-1905) was a man of many talents. He practiced dentistry in Ohio before coming to California in 1849. He mined for a time and earned enough to enter the California College of Physicians and Surgeons in San Francisco, where he obtained his medical degree. He came to Tulare County in 1854 and until his death fifty-one years later he was prominent as a doctor, prospector, county official, patriot and agriculturist. He was constantly on the move and became familiar with the mineral and agricultural possibilities of Tulare, Kern and Inyo counties.

Dr. George practiced medicine sporadically. After 1870 he spent much of his time mining in both Tulare and Inyo counties. He made many trips to and through Death Valley where he had more than one "hair raising" experience, both with people and with the elements. A marker placed in front of his Porterville home tells the story of this remarkable man.

The Dr. Samuel G. George marker is located at his old home, 198 East Mill Street in Porterville.

HERCULES TREE

Hercules Tree, located in Mountain Home State Forest.

Valley residents liked to spend a few weeks each summer camping in the mountains as a respite from the hot weather. Gradually summer resorts where people could get camp sites, meals, supplies and possibly work came into existence.

Camp Lena was such a summer resort. It is now within the Mountain Home State Forest above Springville. One of the first campers there was Jesse Hoskins (1849-1908) of Lindsay.

Mr. Hoskins loved the mountains and the big trees. He was appalled by the wanton destruction of the giants of the forest by lumber companies. In 1887 he filed on eighty acres in order to save some prime trees.

His first summer home was in the heart of a tree he called Hercules. The "room" was twelve feet wide, six feet high at the entrance, and eight feet high at the back. Actually the room had little practical use as sap dripped from the sides and ceiling. Hoskins really lived in a nearby cabin and sold curios to people who came to see the tree.

Jesse Hoskins died in 1908 and his property has been sold several times. Although there has been commercial lumbering in that area since 1956, Hercules and other prime trees have been saved.

HOLLOW LOG

The first recorded visitor in Balch Park was Clinton Brown, who lived near Porterville. He was a sheepman and as was customary took his sheep into the mountains in the summer time. In 1870 he was in what is now Balch Park and camped in a fallen hollow log. He carved the date and his initials into the log, where they are still visible.

Hollow Log, located in Balch Park.

The huge hollow tree undoubtedly had provided shelter for Indians, trappers and prospectors before Clinton Brown came. Fires could be built inside; a small upper opening served as the chimney. John Doyle lived there in 1885 while he built his house. Later he used the log to store apples from his nearby orchard at Doyle's Springs. It was also a center of attraction for campers at Summer Home.

In 1888 the rough end of the log was sawed off and steps were taken to use the log in an unusual way. The Southern Pacific Railroad wanted to use it as a dining car in a promotion plan, but the scheme had to be abandoned because the fallen giant was too big to go through railroad tunnels.

INDIAN ROCK BASINS

This group of Indian Rock Basins is located in Mountain Home State Forest.

Among the riddles left by man or nature are the Indian Rock Basins, popularly called Indian Bathtubs. They are found at high altitudes in the Sierra Nevada, near redwood trees and usually near Indian campsites.

George Stewart, who was among the first to investigate the basins, believed that they were the work of pre-historic people. An excerpt from his papers describes his investigation:

> These cavities measure as a rule from four to five feet in diameter and from one to two feet in depth, and are shaped like huge wash bowls with smoothly curving sides and bottoms... The basins in question are found in groups at altitudes ranging from 4,000 to 9,000 feet, and scattered over an area of about thirty-five miles long from north west to south east in that part of the Sierra

Nevada in Tulare County which is drained by the Kaweah and Tule Rivers.

It was apparent that the basins are of artificial, not of natural origin... The basins in question are readily distinguished from both pot holes and weather pits by the wonderful regularity and perfection of their shapes. Pot holes being literally bored by rotating cobbles tend to assume cylindrical forms and sometimes are broader at the base than at the top, but seldom are shaped like wash bowls; and weather pits expand as a rule laterally more rapidly than downward, and therefore tend to acquire somewhat irregular outlines and flat bottoms.

In 1925 Stewart had found numerous basins in Giant Forest and adjacent areas. They were filled with an accumulation of twigs, leaves and fragments of bark. When he removed the debris, Stewart found bits of charcoal, ashes, humic earth and comminuted granite, and at the bottom he found five or six inches of volcanic ash.

Rock basins are also found in the watershed of the Tule River, on the Middle Fork of the Tule River, on Black Mountain, and in Balch Park. The latter basins were deeper, and Stewart believed that the people who made them may have come from the south and stayed longer than the people from the north.

George Stewart did not guess at a definite use for the basins. To quote again:

It has been suggested to different persons that they may have been used for grinding gold bearing quartz, for tanning hides, for sweat houses, for roasting seeds or meat, for baking pottery, and for storing supplies.

Who are the remarkable people who excavated these basins? At what date did the volcanic eruption take place which put these people to flight? Where did they go? Who are their descendants?

Today, many people believe that the basins were made by natural forces, and they offer convincing proof: During the last glacial period in the Sierra Nevada there were glacial mills or streams of water reaching from the top of the glacier downward. At the bottom of the glacier these mills became powerful twisting forces. The whirling streams were localized for long periods of time and the grinding force on granite produced the basins.

The riddle remains. Why are the basins confined to a small area? Why are they in the redwood belt, and why are they near Indian habitations?

JORDAN TRAIL AND JORDAN TREE

The area in which Balch Park is located was crossed by both the Hockett Trail and the Jordan Trail. The Jordan Trail was built about a year before the Hockett Trail. Both came into being because of the need for better routes from the San Joaquin Valley into Owens Valley.

In 1860 news of a rich strike east of Owens Lake drifted into Visalia. In a few months the Coso mines were attracting hundreds of southern Californians.

John Jordan and his son, William F. Jordan, petitioned the Tulare County Board of Supervisors for a franchise to build a trail and then a wagon road. The petition, dated November 1, 1861, was signed by a long list of prominent men. Jordan proposed to "open a pack trail or passageway leading from Tulare Valley across the mountains to the south end of Big Owens Lake, said trail to commence or start from the county road at George E. Long's residence, passing through Yokohl Valley, and thence easterly across the mountains to the said lake." The trail was to be thirty-three feet wide; construction had to start within one year from the first day of January 1862, and had to be completed within two years. The proposed wagon road had a completion time of five years. The Jordans were franchised to collect tolls on both the trail and wagon road.

John Jordan hired Indians to scout and blaze the trail. The blaze marks which were made with a pole axe and were eight by ten inches on the near and far sides of the trees, lasted for many years.

Work went well and Jordan announced that the trail would open in June 1862. He, his sons William and Silas and several of the crew set out for Visalia. On May 22, 1862 they tried to cross the Kern River on a raft which capsized. John Jordan was the only casualty.

The Jordan Tree is the large tree in the center of this picture, which was taken in 1934 when the family met to dedicate the tree to the memory of John Jordan.

The Jordan Trail was used for many years. The trip from Visalia to Independence took three days. The heaviest travel came during the Civil War when soldiers traveled between Camp Independence and Camp Babbitt in Visalia.

In 1964 descendants of John Jordan met in Balch Park to dedicate the Jordan Tree. The plaque at the base of that magnificent redwood reads:

JOHN JORDAN 1807–1862

THIS GIANT REDWOOD TREE IS DEDICATED TO THE PIONEER SPIRIT OF JOHN JORDAN. DROWNED IN KERN RIVER MAY 22, 1862. HE INITIATED THE TRAIL PROJECT LEADING ACROSS THE SIERRA FROM YOKOHL VALLEY TO THE SOUTHERN END OF BIG OWENS LAKE.

On April 17, 1977, the Jordan family and the Tulare County Historical Society dedicated a marker at the intersection of Highway 198 and the Yokohl Road to mark the Jordan Trail.

The Jordan Trail marker is at the junction of Highway 198 and the Yokohl Valley Road east of Visalia.

JORDAN TOLL TRAIL

THIS MONUMENT IS NEAR THE BEGINNING OF THE JORDAN TRAIL LAID OUT BY JOHN JORDAN IN THE YEAR 1861. THE TRAIL SHORTENED THE ROUTE TO THE SILVER MINES IN THE COSO RANGE NEAR OWEN'S LAKE, EAST OF THE SIERRA NEVADA MOUNTAINS.

THE TRAIL LED UP YOKOHL CREEK, ACROSS THE SOUTH END OF BLUE RIDGE, UP BEAR CREEK TO NEAR BALCH PARK, THENCE TO HOSSACK MEADOW, SOUTH SIDE OF JORDAN PEAK, KERN FLAT ON KERN RIVER AND CROSSED THE MAIN SUMMIT OF THE SIERRA VIA JORDAN HOT SPRINGS AND MONACHE MEADOW.

THE TRAIL DOWN THE EAST SLOPE WAS BY OLANCHA PASS, DOWN WALKER'S CREEK AND TO OWEN'S LAKE. PORTIONS OF THE TRAIL ARE STILL IN USE.

THIS MARKER PLACED BY MEMBERS OF THE JORDAN FAMILY AND THE TULARE COUNTY HISTORICAL SOCIETY.

THIS PLATE CAST BY RONALD E. LOVING
GREAT-GREAT GRANDSON OF JOHN JORDAN

OLD STAGE ROAD

This marker commemorating traveled routes in the lower valley was placed at present day Fountain Springs. The original springs are about a mile and a half northwest.

Old Stage Road marker, at Fountain Springs east of Ducor on Avenue 56.

OLD STAGE ROAD

RUNNING NORTH AND SOUTH FOLLOWING AN OLDER INDIAN TRAIL IS THE ROUTE TAKEN BY MANY SPANISH EXPEDITIONS, AMERICAN TRAPPERS, TRADERS AND PARTIES OF EXPLORATION. IT WAS THE MAJOR INLAND ROUTE OF GOLD SEEKERS TO THE NORTHERN AND SOUTHERN MINES AND WAS THE FIRST PUBLIC ROAD IN TULARE COUNTY. ONE OF THE MOST NOTEWORTHY SPANISH EXPEDITIONS WAS THE GABRIEL MORAGA EXPEDITION OF 1806 EXPLORING THE AREA SOUTH FROM THE MISSION SAN JUAN BAUTISTA THROUGH TEJON PASS TO MISSION SAN FERNANDO. MORAGA NAMED THE SAN JOAQUIN RIVER FROM WHICH THE VALLEY DERIVES ITS NAME. SOME OF THE MORE FAMOUS AMERICAN PARTIES TO PASS THIS WAY WERE:

JEDEDIAH S. SMITH	1826-1827
EWING YOUNG	1830-1832
THOMAS "PEG LEG" SMITH	1830s AND LATER
JOSEPH R. WALKER	1830s AND LATER
JOHN C. FREMONT WITH KIT CARSON AS GUIDE	1844
EDWARD KERN, JOSEPH R. WALKER AS GUIDE, DETACHED FROM FREMONT'S 3RD EXPEDITION	1845
STOCKTON-LOS ANGELES ROAD	1853
BUTTERFIELD OVERLAND STAGE	1858 TO 1861

MARKER PLACED BY
TULARE COUNTY BICENTENNIAL COMMISSION
IN COOPERATION WITH
TULARE COUNTY HISTORICAL SOCIETY
OCTOBER 24, 1976

PLANO

Plano and Vandalia were once thriving communities adjacent to the Tule River. Both predated Porterville, which grew as they disappeared. Vandalia suffered from the ravages of the 1862 flood and was the first to fade into history, although the name still exists as the name of a school, a bridge and a cemetery.

Plano was on higher ground and did not suffer so much in the flood. It was also on the main stage road and attracted business establishments. The wording on the plaque relates the story of Plano:

PLANO

THIS SITE OVERLOOKS THE FORMER PIONEER VILLAGE OF PLANO. FIRST SETTLED IN 1861 BY A WAGON TRAIN OF SETTLERS FROM TEXAS WHO FOLLOWED THE BUTTERFIELD STAGE ROUTE WEST, THIS TOWN BECAME A WAY STATION ON THE STAGE ROUTES OF THE 1860'S. FOR A TIME WAS THE MAJOR TRADING CENTER OF SOUTHEASTERN TULARE COUNTY AND WAS THE COUNTY'S THIRD LARGEST COMMUNITY. HERE WERE CHURCHES, STORES, HOTELS, JUSTICE COURT, BLACKSMITH, BRICK KILN, SALOONS, LIVERY STABLE, AND PACKING HOUSE. ALSO TULE RIVER COUNTRY'S ONLY SCHOOL, POST OFFICE AND PERMANENT CEMETERY. AT ONE TIME THE EARLY CAMPBELL-MORELAND DITCH BROUGHT WATER TO THE AREA AND HERE DEVELOPED THE FIRST COMMERCIAL ORANGE GROVE IN THE VALLEY. THE VILLAGE REMAINED ACTIVE UNTIL ABOUT 1915.

TULARE COUNTY HISTORICAL SOCIETY
MAY 25, 1975

The Plano marker is two miles south of Porterville on Plano Street.

PORTERVILLE'S FIRST CHURCH

Porterville's first church, the First United Methodist Church, was located on the corner of Putnam and Fourth streets. It is now the First Missionary Baptist Church.

The first Protestant minister to serve in the Tule River country was the Reverend John K. McKelvey (1830-1897), a circuit rider for the Methodist Church. His circuit extended from Mariposa to Los Angeles. He established the Visalia Methodist Church in 1858, and the Tule River Charge was established the next year. The congregation met in Plano at the home of David Campbell. A small church built at the junction of Plano Road and Vandalia Avenue in 1863 was later moved to property donated by James Martin, Sr.

In 1873-74 the Tule River Charge was renamed the Plano Charge and it included Porterville. Porterville began to eclipse Plano in growth so a Methodist Church was built in Porterville in 1869. By 1871 most members who lived in Plano or Vandalia had transferred their memberships to Porterville.

In 1906 a church dominated by a huge dome skylight was built on East Putnam Street. Over the years alterations and additions have changed the appearance of the church but the skylight is still a dominant feature. The building was sold to another denomination and presently the United First Methodist Church is located on East Morton Street.

The McKelvey family were prominent in county history. The Reverend John K. McKelvey founded Methodist churches in Visalia, Porterville, Plano, Hanford, Chinese Camp, Mariposa, Stockton, Eel River and Ukiah. His parents, John and Mary McKelvey, owned the Plano Hotel. His brother George was Porterville's first postmaster. His brother Chris married Nellie Carothers, his sister Mary married John Tyler, and another sister, Eliza, married Andrew Mapes. McKelvey's son, J. Addison McKelvey, carried on his father's ministry.

PORTERVILLE FLOUR MILL

Grist mills were an important factor in pioneer days, for they ground flour, corn meal, and feed for poultry and stock. In 1854 the Matthews brothers were operating a grist mill in Visalia, and in 1865 there was a grist mill northwest of present day Exeter.

The first grist mill in the Tule River country dates back to 1868 when trustees of the Tule River Ditch Company sold the water power of the ditch for one dollar. The buyers were John Fleck and Henry Clark, who had to build a flouring mill within six months. Fleck and Clark built the mill and sold it to T. P. Johnson, J. Patrick Murray and John Keeney. They paid $5,000 for it and Keeney went to work as the miller. Ownership changed several times, and during the dry cycle of the 1870s there was not enough river water to power the mill at times.

In 1882 Charles McLean and Arthur Abbey bought the mill and replaced the burr stones with bolting machinery. The flour was sold under the name New Process Roller Flour. Six years later the Pioneer Land Company bought the mill for the water rights and built a generating plant south of the mill which produced enough electricity to light the principal streets of Porterville.

In 1889 John and Hiram Manter bought the mill and hired Andrew Leslie as millwright. In 1897 Mr. Leslie bought the mill

First park and flour mill in Porterville.

and replaced it with a three-story building and steam operated machinery. He operated the mill until 1912. By that time most people were buying nationally advertised flour and other staples.

George Murray, son of J. P. Murray, deeded nine acres of the property to the City of Porterville, stipulating that it be developed as a park. Henry Hunsaker deeded two acres and the Pioneer Land Company donated nineteen acres. The park was named Burbank Park. After George Murray died in 1918 the name was changed to Murray Park.

Probably the park feature which aroused the most interest was the old three-story mill. In 1929, Dr. Will Leslie, son of Andrew Leslie, donated the mill property to the city, but little was done to preserve the landmark. Many people believed that it was haunted. It continued to be a part of Porterville's history until, unfortunately, it was torn down in 1938.

The Porterville Flour Mill marker is on East Putnam Avenue between Plano Street and Leggett Drive.

SITE OF PORTERVILLE FLOUR MILL

FROM 1868 TO 1912 FLOUR GRIST MILLS OPERATED ON THIS SITE, WHICH WERE VERY IMPORTANT TO THIS AREA. USING AN EXTENSION OF A DITCH FROM THE MONACHE RESERVATION TO PROVIDE WATER POWER, DUG BY INDIAN LABOR IN 1863, WITH WATER TAKEN FROM THE TULE RIVER FIVE MILES UPSTREAM, THE FIRST MILL WAS BUILT BY JOHN FLECK AND HENRY CLARK TO GRIND GRAIN PRODUCED IN THE SURROUNDING AREA AND TO PROVIDE FOOD FOR THIS COMMUNITY. IN AUGUST 1863 THE MILL OPERATION WAS SOLD TO T. P. JOHNSON AND JOHN KEELEY AND LATER TO J. P. MURRAY. THE MILL WAS OWNED IN 1876 BY ALBERT HENRY, OPERATED BY HIS NEPHEW WILLSHIRE HENRY. IN THE 1880'S THE REMODELED MILL WAS RUN BY MR. McLEAN AND A. A. ABBEY. THE PIONEER LAND COMPANY PURCHASED THE DITCH PROPERTY AND MILL IN 1888 AND JOHN T. MANTER RENTED IT. HE HIRED ANDREW LESLIE AS A MILLWRIGHT WHO BOUGHT OUT THE BUSINESS. IN 1897 HE CONSTRUCTED A THREE STORY MODERN BRICK FLOUR MILL RUN BY STEAM POWER. IN 1929, AFTER THE MILLING OPERATION CLOSED, WILL LESLIE DEEDED THE PROPERTY TO THE CITY AND IN 1938 THE MILL BUILDING WAS TORN DOWN AND THE SITE INCLUDED IN MURRAY PARK.

TULARE COUNTY HISTORICAL SOCIETY   APRIL 25, 1976

Royal Porter Putnam's store and home, about 1866.

PORTER PUTNAM'S HOME AND STORE

Royal Porter Putnam (1837-1889) was twenty years of age when he came to California. He was miserably ill on the overland trip and recuperated in Los Angeles. He knew he could not mine so he took a northbound stage to look for other work. By the time he arrived in Visalia he had a job as a Butterfield agent at the Packwood Station northwest of present Strathmore. In 1859 he was sent to the larger Tule River Station where meals and overnight accommodations for travelers were sketchy but available.

Young Putnam saved enough from his monthly thirty dollars to put in supplies to sell to travelers, Indians and settlers. People who came to the station began to call it Porter's place, since he preferred to use his middle name.

The Butterfield stages were discontinued in 1861 but Porter Putnam stayed. In 1862 a devastating flood changed the history of the Tule River country. After the water had subsided, Tule River was flowing about a mile south of the old channel. Vandalia was heavily damaged in the same flood. Putnam moved to higher ground south of the station and paid $200 for forty acres of land between the old and new Tule River channels. He built a two-story combination home, store and inn. The store was on the ground floor, rooms were on the second story, and a lean-to served as the kitchen. Thrifty Putnam built the partitions from the packing cases in which his merchandise arrived. Today, Putnam's building would be on the northeast corner of Main and Oak streets in Porterville.

Putnam had his forty acres surveyed into town lots which he offered free to anyone who would move from nearby Plano or Vandalia. For a time he had no takers but an epidemic of malaria made higher ground look attractive and people began to come. At first the village was called Putnamville, then it became Portersville (later changed to Porterville).

In the 1880s a movement to create new counties from existing counties swept California. One of several proposed in Tulare County was Putnam County with Porterville as its county seat. Although most of the bills did not pass in the state legislature, one that did resulted in the formation of Kings County from western Tulare County in 1893.

Putnam's first home and store are marked with these plaques:

HERE WAS PORTER'S PLACE: HOTEL AND STORE OF R. PORTER PUTNAM IN 1861. THE BEGINNING OF THE TOWN OF PORTERVILLE. FIRST SURVEYED IN 1864, AND INCORPORATED IN 1902 AS THE CITY OF PORTERVILLE.

ERECTED BY THE HISTORICAL COMMITTEE
CITY OF PORTERVILLE
1955

The Putnam House and Store marker is on the northeast corner of Main and Oak streets in Porterville. Shown at the dedication of the marker are, left to right, Miss Ina Stiner, Howard Frame and Mayor L. H. Hamilton.

The second marker is at the Putnam home, Mill and Third streets.

HOME OF
ROYAL PORTER PUTNAM
BUILT IN 1866 AT 165 NORTH MAIN STREET
AND MOVED TO THIS SITE IN 1888.

THIS MONUMENT DONATED BY THE
WESTFIELD SCHOOL UNDER THE AUSPICES OF
THE BICENTENNIAL COMMITTEE
MAY 1975

SODA SPRINGS (SPRINGVILLE)

Soda Springs.

Soda Springs in Springville.

The Yaudanchi tribe ranged along the upper Tule River where evidences of their villages are still visible. The Yokuts were well aware of springs and were knowledgeable about those with medicinal qualities. It is evident that they used the spring water at California Hot Springs and the soda springs in what is now Springville.

In 1864 John Crabtree homesteaded the 160 acres which included the soda springs and later sold to people who hoped to buld a health resort. They did build a boarding house which was later used as a hotel, but the resort did not materialize. There were other owners including such well-known pioneers as O. H. P. Duncan, S. Sweet and Avon Coburn.

William Daunt had settled in the area in 1860 and the community which grew up around his lumber mill was called Daunt. Daunt was granted a postoffice February 18, 1886. In 1911 the Porterville Northeastern Railroad reached Daunt and brought in more people and more business. The nearby soda springs were used extensively during that time and a name which had some connection with them seemed more appropriate than Daunt, so the town became Springville, January 24, 1911.

The effervescent spring water was always an attraction for picnickers. In the days before bottled and canned beverages, it was customary to bring fruit juices to add to the soda water, much to the delight of the children. From time to time attempts were made to bottle the water for commercial use.

The springs are still there, but are on private property.

HOME OF INA STINER

Miss Ina Stiner (1875-1967), teacher, biographer and historian, came to Porterville in 1912. She taught English at Porterville High School until the new campus was opened on Olive Avenue in 1923. From 1923 until her retirement in 1938 she served as high school librarian.

The house at 191 North E Street in which she and her mother lived was moved from Plano to Porterville in the 1920s. For fifty years before that, the house had been the Plano Presbyterian manse.

The memorial plaque in front of the house reads:

> FORMER HOME SITE
> OF
> INA STINER
> PORTERVILLE'S FOREMOST HISTORIAN
>
> FORMER PRESBYTERIAN MANSE
> ORIGINALLY BUILT IN PLANO
>
> TULARE COUNTY
> HISTORICAL SOCIETY
> JANUARY 18, 1976

TAILHOLT

Tailholt, once a thriving mining camp, came into existence during the Kern River gold rush of the early 1850s. It was located on White River fifteen miles southeast of Ducor. Today it is a ghost town. There had been prospectors along White River as early as 1853 when DeWitt C. Biggs and Andrew J. Maltby located what became the productive Keyes Mine. David B. James was prospecting on Greenhorn Mountain at about the same time.

The first mining camp on White River was Dogtown, about a mile and a half south of State Registered Landmark Number 413. A road hacked into the mines by-passed Dogtown, so the miners packed their tents and tools and moved upstream.

Whimsical names such as Dogtown and Tailholt were common during the early mining days in California. As time passed so did the stories of the derivations of the names. Several versions of the origin of the name Tailholt have survived. According to one version, one of the miners owned a cow. He made a pet of the animal, which followed him everywhere. When he drank too much he would hang on to the tail of the faithful bovine, who guided him home. One night a fellow miner saw him staggering by and yelled, "Hang on brother, a tailholts better'n no holt a'tall."

When a postoffice was granted June 10, 1862, Levi Mitchell was appointed postmaster and was asked to submit a name. He thought White River was more dignified than Tailholt.

White River could trace its name back to that remarkable

priest, Father Francisco Garces, who explored the southern valley in 1776. On May 3 he found a pretty little stream which he called Rio de la Santa Cruz. Years later an unrecorded Spaniard changed the name to Rio Blanco, or White River.

Tailholt (White River) prospered, and miners, merchants, farmers, stockmen and teamsters made a good living. Over a million dollars in gold was mined out. More important was the fact that mines along Kern River, White River and the gulches brought an estimated sixty-nine hundred persons into Tulare County. Not all of them stayed, for this was not pick, pan and water mining. The gold was buried in quartz, and it was necessary to dig shafts and tunnels to reach the lodes. That in turn made it necessary to have arrastras or stamp mills to crush the quartz to recover the gold. These procedures were expensive, and when the price of gold went down around 1900, the mines were closed. Tailholt gradually became a ghost town.

An observant visitor will still see traces of the past. There are prospect holes, collapsed shafts and tunnels, tailings and trees which once grew near homes. There are two cemeteries. The one on the north hillside is the community cemetery. Boothill is on a south side hill.

The Tailholt marker is in White River, some fifteen miles east of Ducor.

In 1949 some three thousand people came to Tailholt to dedicate a memorial marker.

TAILHOLT

TAILHOLT BEGAN AS A GOLD MINING CAMP ABOUT 1856. DURING THE KERN RIVER GOLD RUSH GOLD WAS OBTAINED FROM PLACER AND SHAFT OPERATIONS. MINING HAS BEEN CARRIED OUT INTERMITTENTLY SINCE THE TIME OF DISCOVERY. DURING PERIODS OF ACTIVITY THERE HAS BEEN A CONSIDERABLE SETTLEMENT HERE. THE NAME WAS CHANGED TO WHITE RIVER ABOUT 1870.

MARKER PLACED BY THE
CALIFORNIA CENTENNIAL COMMISSION
BASE FURNISHED BY THE TULARE COUNTY HISTORICAL SOCIETY

DEDICATED MAY 15, 1949

TULE RIVER INDIAN RESERVATION

In 1851-52 the United States sent treaty commissioners to California. They made treaties with 120 tribes and sub-tribes, promising the Indians goods and services in return for relinquishing their land. The treaties caused such a furor in California that they were rejected by the United States Senate on June 8, 1852 and placed in a secret file where they remained until 1905.

Although the treaties were rejected, the federal government was not unaware of the plight of the Indians. In 1852 General Edward F. Beale arrived in California to establish five reservations. He set up only one, the Sebastian Reserve near Tejon Pass. There were also "farms" on the Kings and Fresno rivers.

The Tule River War of 1856 focused attention on that area, and the Tule River Indian Reservation was established in 1857. It was about a mile south of Porterville in what is now the Alta School District. The reservation was not surveyed immediately and in 1857 Thomas Madden used school warrants to file on 1,289 acres of the same land. It became known as the Madden Farm and the federal government paid him rent until 1876. In 1881 Madden sold his farm to Elias Jacob for $1,000.

The reservation was too close to Porterville, where unscrupulous men sold whiskey to the Indians. In 1870 some drunken

This marker is on the site of the first reservation, now the grounds of the Alta Vista School in southeast Porterville.

Indians brutally murdered Mrs. Jesse Bonsall and her two small children in Plano. Two of the men were caught and lynched.

Federal officials came to Porterville in response to the demand to move the reservation. They were guided into the mountains east of Porterville by Huffum White, a local stockman. The site selected for the new reservation was within the drainage basin of the South Fork of the Tule River and far back into the foothills (the present reservation). The report stated that there were thousands of acres of tillable land, but 500 would have been more realistic.

In 1873 the Indians were ordered to move to the new reservation, but the old one was not closed until 1876. The agent reported that Indians from the Tule, Tejon, Wuchumne, Kaweah, Kings, River and Monache tribes were moved. As nearly as he could ascertain, approximately one thousand people were involved in the exodus.

Early agents for both reservations were: Cage Tucker, 1859; George Hoffman, 1863-67; Charles Maltby, 1867-69; Lieutenant John Purcell, 1869-70; John W. Miller, 1870-71; Charles Maltby, 1871-73; Joel B. Vosburg, 1873-75; Charles G. Belnap, 1875-86.

The first reservation had a complex of adobe buildings used for administrative purposes. Dr. Samuel George and later on Dr.

Franklin Whaley visited the reservation weekly, and Lt. Purcell's wife started a school in 1869. Overseers taught farming and the Indians raised foodstuffs as well as grain.

The early overseers were local men: John D. Tyler, 1859; Origen Wilcox, 1860; Ralph Carroll, 1861; John Loyd, 1862; William Thompson, 1877.

The adobe buildings stood for many years. As they began to disintegrate, the fig trees planted by the main building seemed to grow larger. These trees also had a history. John W. Williams, a participant in the Bear Flag Rebellion and later Visalia City marshal, brought the fig cuttings from Fort Tejon in 1860. They were the first fig trees planted in Tulare County.

All that is left to locate the first reservation is a marker placed on the grounds of the Alta Vista School.

TULE RIVER INDIAN RESERVATION

A RESERVATION WAS ORIGINALLY ESTABLISHED IN 1857. INDIANS FROM A WIDESPREAD AREA WERE BROUGHT HERE. THE NATIVES OF THIS VICINITY WERE THE KOYETI TRIBE TOWARD THE WEST AND THE YAUDANCHI TRIBE TOWARD THE EAST. BOTH WERE BRANCHES OF THE YOKUTS INDIANS THAT OCCUPIED THE SAN JOAQUIN VALLEY.

THIS LOCATION NOT PROVING SATISFACTORY, THE TULE RIVER INDIAN RESERVATION WAS MOVED TO ITS PRESENT LOCATION TEN MILES SOUTHEAST IN 1873.

MARKER PLACED BY THE CALIFORNIA CENTENNIAL COMMISSION
BASE FURNISHED BY THE TULARE COUNTY HISTORICAL SOCIETY
STATE REGISTERED LANDMARK #388
DEDICATED OCTOBER 16, 1949

TULE RIVER SCHOOL DISTRICT

The Tule River School District, organized February 5, 1861, was the first school district in southern Tulare County. The modest school building was located about 200 yards south of the Tule River stage crossing on the east side of the old stage road. James Logsdon was the first teacher, and he may have taught in his home before the district was organized. The first trustees of record were David Campbell, Deming Gibbons and William Martin.

The teacher had a desk, but the children sat on logs. They considered their lot much improved when the logs were fitted with "legs" which raised them to a more comfortable height. Since there was no bell, the teacher called the pupils together by rapping on the wall with a willow switch. Presumably the switch also had other uses!

In 1865 the men hauled in lumber and built what became known as the Clapboard School. The people made the furniture by hand. Two children sat at each desk, and a long recitation bench was in the front of the room near the stove.

The dissension generated by the Civil War spilled into the school, just as it did in Visalia. Some parents even removed their children from school. Students explained poor grades by saying the teacher was a Republican and "had it in" for children whose parents were Democrats.

In 1870, Porterville organized its own school. Five years later the Tule River District joined the Porterville School District, and the Clapboard School became the Plano School and later the Vandalia School. That name was used until 1925, when Vandalia School joined the Porterville Elementary School District.

VANDALIA

The village of Vandalia, adjacent to Tule River, lasted only a few years but its name has remained as part of the county's history. The first settlers came in 1859, many of them from Illinois, and they named their community for the town of Vandalia in that state.

Vandalia enjoyed a favorable location on the north-south road through the valley. Although most settlers raised stock, the soil gave promise of future farms. The nearby Tule River School was organized in February 1861, and the postoffice, granted on April 29, 1859, was built across the river in an area which would become Porterville.

People did not plan on the capricious forces of nature, however. The terrible flood of 1862 not only washed away much soil in the village but moved the Tule River channel. Gradually, people relocated to higher ground to make a living or to escape ague (malaria).

The name Vandalia remains in use today—by a school, cemetery and irrigation district.

This marker is located on the grounds of the Vandalia School in Porterville.

WOODVILLE SCHOOL

The area west of Porterville, which was well-supplied with grammar schools, reflected the desire of residents for schools "of their own" near their homes. The schools served as centers for social events and often doubled as churches on Sunday. To meet the varied needs of their patrons, the school buildings were sometimes moved from one location to another.

County records for the Woodville area date from 1881. School registers, deeds and personal recollections provide dates of the organization of early schools.

In the 1892 Thompson Atlas, five schools are shown in townships 21 and 22 and ranges 24, 25 and 26. They were Rockford, organized in 1868; Surprise and Pleasant View, 1876; Woodville, 1878; and Hanby, 1884.

The Woodville school marker commemorates the centennial of the district:

WOODVILLE SCHOOL

WOODVILLE SCHOOL FOUNDED IN 1881
TULARE COUNTY HISTORICAL SOCIETY
MAY 24, 1981

The Woodville School marker is located on the grounds of the Woodville Veterans Memorial Building.

THE ZALUD HOUSE

John Zalud (1851-1944) came to the United States from his native Bohemia, as did his wife, Mary Jane Herdlika Zalud. Three years after arriving in San Francisco in 1872, the Zaluds moved to a new railroad town called Tulare. Both good cooks, they opened the Delmonico Restaurant and catered to railroad people. But in 1890, Tulare lost its largest source of income when the Southern Pacific Railroad moved its shops and roundhouse to Bakersfield.

The Zaluds then moved to Porterville where John's brother, Anton Zalud, lived. In 1890, John Zalud opened a saloon on Main Street next door to Scotty's Chophouse. Both places operated on a twenty-four-hour schedule. A good businessman, Zalud invested his saloon earnings in land and cattle.

The family home on the corner of Morton and Hockett streets was built in the French style. It featured innovative construction

The Zalud House, on the corner of Morton and Hockett streets in Porterville.

in its double walls with insulating air space. The house was and still is a show place.

The Zaluds raised three of their seven children. Anna (1872-1972) married William H. Brooks and lived in the Brooks mansion in Los Angeles. Edward Zalud (1877-1922) was killed when he and his horse fell in a riding accident.

Pearle (1884-1970) completed her education at the New England Conservatory of Music in Boston. From 1904 until 1911 she taught music in the Zalud home. Her mother died in 1912, and from then on Pearle's life was devoted to her father, her music, and her garden. Pearle and her father traveled around the world several times, collecting many of the art objects now displayed in the Zalud house.

The elder Zaluds started the garden in 1892, gradually creating a beautiful formal cultivated area. Roses predominated, but in the spring and fall the garden offered visitors a mass of color as bulbs and annuals bloomed. It was described in garden magazines and newspaper stories and pictured in the "Pictorial Guide to American Gardens."

In her will, Pearle Zalud left land in Porterville for a park to be named for Edward Zalud. She left the house, its contents and a substantial amount of money to the City of Porterville to be used as a museum in memory of her parents.

The bequest is administered by trustees. They have aided the curator, Mrs. Hannah Schultz, in restoring, repairing and arranging the house and its contents. The Zalud house is used for special events, musicals and tours. A small fee is asked for its maintenance.

Part 4
Historic Sites in the Southwest Portion of Tulare County

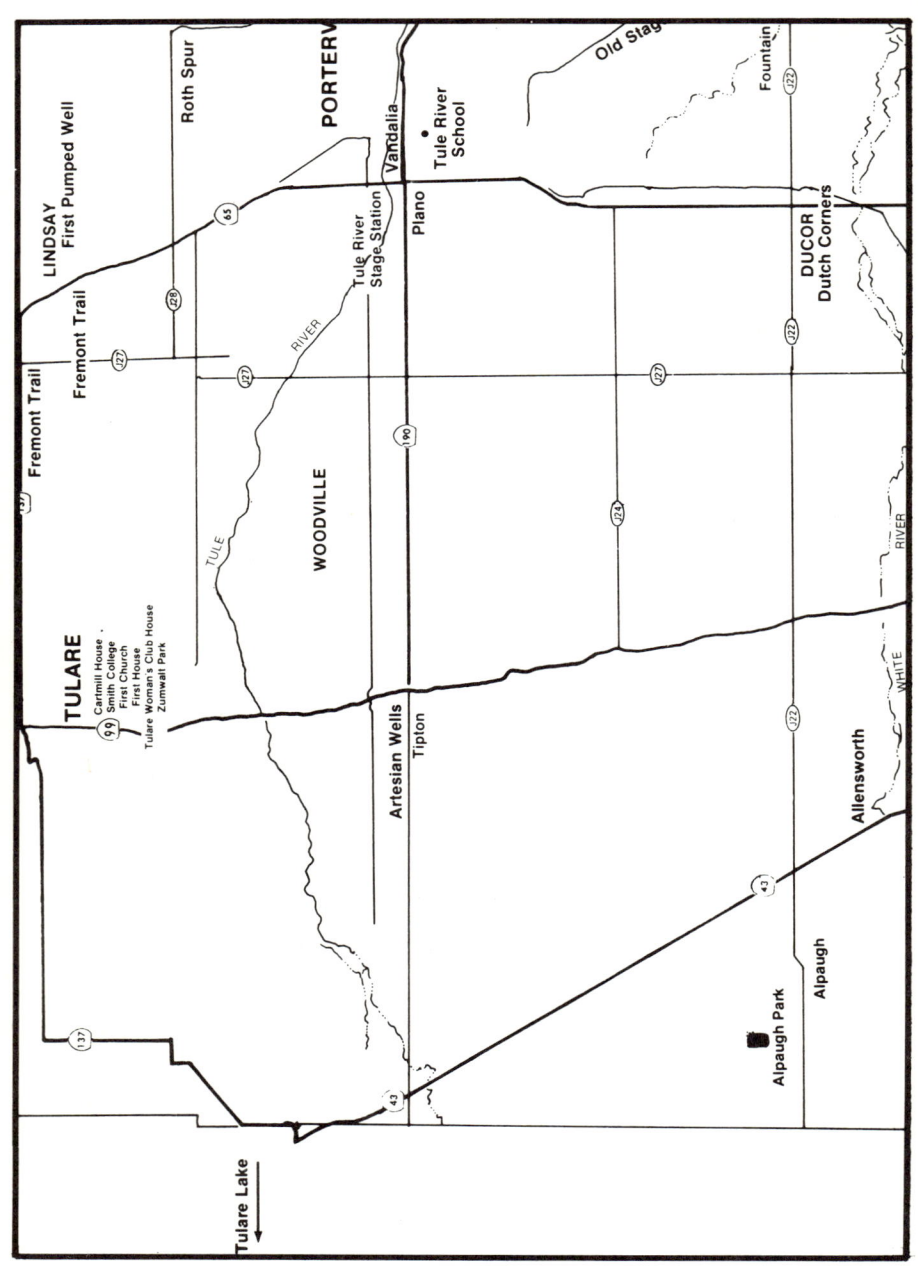

Historic Sites in the Southwest Portion of Tulare County

ALLENSWORTH

Allensworth was started by Allan Allensworth (1842-1914), born a slave and twice sold on the auction block. He escaped from his owner and enlisted in the Union Army, serving during the Civil War. After a religious conversion, he returned to the army as a chaplain in the all-black Twenty-fourth Infantry. He saw service in the Spanish-American War and the Philippine Insurrection and left the army as Lieutenant Colonel Allensworth, the army's highest ranking black soldier.

He had dreamed of an all-black community where black people could prove their worth, and he began to interest friends in his plan. They formed a company and in 1909 bought several thousand acres in southwestern Tulare County. By 1912 some two thousand acres had been sold for small farms. Colonel Allensworth had planned to name the community Solita, but the people insisted that it bear his name.

The restored home of Colonel and Mrs. Allan Allensworth in Allensworth.

Allensworth grew and prospered. It soon had a school, church, post office, newspaper, cemetery, and its own judicial district. The farms produced alfalfa, sugar beets, grain and vegetables. There were dairies, apiaries and poultry farms.

But all was not well. Heavy irrigation percolated alkali to the surface of the ground and the same water that had turned the plains into lush fields began to kill vegetation. Gradually, well water became so impregnated with minerals it was not fit for household use.

In 1914, Colonel Allensworth was killed in a vehicle accident in southern California. The combination of his death and the water problem doomed the community. Families drifted away, land went for back taxes, and the depression took its toll.

The community slowly died, but Colonel Allensworth's dream did not die. After years of planning, in 1969 the state took steps to restore Allensworth. The California State Legislature allocated funds and designated the community as Colonel Allensworth State Historical Park. The long-range plan seeks to restore and replace the original buildings and establish Allensworth as a center for historical, cultural and interpretative black studies.

ARTESIAN WATER AND THE TREE RANCH

Artesian water comes from underground strata which are under enough pressure to force water upward without pumping. The flow is measured by the amount of water which comes out of the pipe, spilling in all directions.

In 1877 the Southern Pacific Railroad had a well bored about two miles south of Tipton. An artesian strata was found at a depth of 310 feet. The four-inch flow was diverted into an artificial lake which was stocked with carp. Blue gum trees, locust trees, fruit trees, flowers and shrubs made the spot an oasis on the dry plains. A nursery which provided trees to be planted along the railroad right of way gave the place its name, Tree Ranch.

In 1881 artesian water was found on the Paige and Morton Ranch three miles west of Tulare. A. J. Cromley, who used a divining rod, located the site. The discovery was so important

Artesian well located near Artesia, south of Waukena. Artesia is now in Kings County.

that an elaborate ceremony was held to dedicate the well, which was named the Enterprise. Coins were tossed into the pipe and a liberal amount of whiskey was also poured down it. One account said the name should be changed to Temperance Well, because the coins and the whiskey were promptly ejected.

An artesian strata twenty-five miles long and fifteen miles wide was developed along the axis of the valley. It included Hanford, Armona, Grangeville, Lemoore, Tulare, Goshen, Earlimart, Pixley and Tipton. By 1885 there were 250 artesian wells in the county, all of which helped develop the semi-arid west side for agriculture.

Artesian water stopped flowing in the first decade of this century. Some said it coincided with the fact that Tulare Lake was completely dry. Others attributed it to the 1906 earthquake. Whatever the reason, standpipes were capped and other sources of water had to be found.

GEORGE STOCKTON BERRY

After the Southern Pacific Railroad was built down the valley in 1872, the availability of bulk transportation changed the base of the valley's economy from livestock to cereal grains. That in turn called for better farm machinery. Old machinery was improved upon or new was invented by valley farmers. The Stockton Gang Plow replaced the single share plow, better harrows and seeders were made, and the Fresno Scraper moved tons of earth, but the invention that was to revolutionize farming machinery was the Berry Steam Harvester, created near Lindsay in 1886.

George Stockton Berry, who farmed 2,000 acres near Lindsay with his brother William, sought some mechanical method to alleviate two serious problems connected with grain farming. One was the loss of livestock which died from summer heat and the effort of pulling the huge harvesters. The other was the disposition of straw left after harvest.

Mr. Berry's machine was built around a steam engine used to operate a stationary thresher. The parts which he designed were made in Visalia; the machine was put together in Benecia and shipped to Tulare. To be used as a harvester, the steam operated machine ran in reverse. By easy manipulation of parts, it could be run forward and used as a tractor to pull plows. Eleven men made up the crew.

Mr. Berry used the cheapest and most available fuel—the straw left in the field. He put lanterns on the harvester and operated on a twenty-four-hour basis. Several more harvesters, with an average price tag of $7,000 each, were ordered by other farmers, and the invention drew visitors from all parts of the state.

Mr. Berry patented some of the parts of the steam harvester but not the differential gear, which is one of the basic tools of the automotive industry. He sold his patents to Daniel Best of San Leandro, who manufactured a wide line of farm machinery. In 1925 the Best Company merged with the Holt Company of Stockton under the name Caterpillar Tractor Company. Modern tractors as well as tanks used in warfare are descendants of

The George Stockton Berry marker is located on the Lindsay High School campus, former site of the Berry ranch. On the right is Erma Osborn Lantrip, granddaughter of Berry. On the left is Karen Lantrip, great-granddaughter of Berry.

George Stockton Berry's revolutionary invention.

George S. Berry was also interested in civic matters and was elected to the state assembly in 1888 and to the state senate in 1890. The land on which his home was built included the present Lindsay High School. The house was removed when the school was built. The Tulare County Historical Society dedicated a marker on that site in 1978:

GEORGE STOCKTON BERRY

BORN IN MISSOURI IN 1847, BERRY CAME TO PLACERVILLE, CALIFORNIA IN 1857. HE FARMED NEAR MODESTO AND GRANGEVILLE. IN 1875 HE BOUGHT TWO THOUSAND ACRES OF RAILROAD LAND AND ESTABLISHED HIS HOME AND RANCH HEADQUARTERS NEAR THIS MONUMENT.

IN 1865-66 BERRY CONVERTED HIS PORTABLE STEAM ENGINE INTO A TRACTOR, AND MOUNTED HARVESTING MACHINERY ON IT TO MAKE THE FIRST SELF-PROPELLED COMBINE HARVESTER. IN LATER YEARS THE HEADER WAS EXTENDED TO CUT A FORTY FOOT SWATH. STRAW WAS USED FOR FUEL. IN THE FALL AND WINTER THE TRACTOR WAS USED FOR PLOWING.

A NUMBER OF MACHINES WERE BUILT FOR BERRY BY THE BENECIA AGRICULTURAL WORKS AND WERE SOLD TO FARMERS IN THE CENTRAL VALLEY. HE SOLD HIS PATENT TO DANIEL BEST OF SAN LEANDRO. IN 1925 THE BEST COMPANY AND HOLT BROTHERS MERGED TO FORM THE CATERPILLAR TRACTOR COMPANY.

BERRY WAS AMONG THE FIRST TO PLANT ORANGES AND OLIVES IN THE LINDSAY AREA AND HAD A VINEYARD. HE WAS A MEMBER OF THE ASSEMBLY IN 1888 AND WAS ELECTED TO THE STATE SENATE IN 1890. HE WAS A MEMBER OF THE LINDSAY SCHOOL BOARD IN THE 1890s.

STOCKTON BERRY DIED DECEMBER 12, 1917.

TULARE COUNTY HISTORICAL SOCIETY
MARCH 12, 1978

CARTMILL HOUSE (TULARE)

The house at 304 West Tulare Street is the home of Miss Mary Cartmill, granddaughter of Dr. William Cartmill (1822-1906). Cartmill is credited with laying the foundation of Tulare County's multi-million dollar dairy industry.

His son, Wooster B. Cartmill (1857-1938), built and operated the first creamery in Tulare.

Dr. Cartmill came to California in 1849. He mined and practiced medicine at times, but like many other forty-niners found

The Cartmill house, located at 304 West Tulare Street, was built by W. F. Cartmill in 1873.

that operating a general store was more productive than digging for gold. In 1855, he went back east to marry Miss Sophia Barnes (1833-1907). When they returned to California, they found that Dr. Cartmill's partner had sold the business and decamped with the money.

Dr. Cartmill recouped his losses by buying good milk cows. In order to find good pasture land, he came to the southern San Joaquin Valley. Finding what he wanted, he moved his family to an area of what is now Tulare, in 1861. He drove a herd of 100 cows to the ranch, and fortune seemed to smile on the family. Their initial prosperity did not last long, however, for the herd was spooked and only a few cows were found. The process of building up the herd had to start all over.

The principal product of the Cartmill dairy, butter, was sold in Visalia and to people going to the mines along White River, Kern River, and Owens Valley.

In 1873 the Cartmills built the house on Tulare Street so the children could attend school in Tulare. It is a well-kept reminder of a period of gracious living.

FIRST PUMPED WELL

John J. Cairns (1844-1926), bonanza wheat grower of the valley, believed that water could be pumped from beneath the surface of the plains. Many of his contemporaries scoffed at the idea of a water table. In fact, stockmen were convinced that nothing would grow on the plains. Somehow they overlooked the verdant wild grasses on which their cattle fed. The few people who tried to raise grain were called sandlappers and sky farmers.

In 1890 Mr. Cairns bought a ten horsepower Byron Jackson centrifugal pump. He had been thinking of planting oranges on his ranch west of Lindsay and wanted a dependable supply of water. He planned to put a pump in each corner of a twenty-foot-square brick-lined pit dug by his workmen. Power for the pumps would come from a steam thresher engine.

The output of water from the first well exceeded everyone's expectations. Mr. Cairns had not only proved the existence of a water table but in so doing had changed the economy of the lower valley.

Farmers started digging wells and buying pumps. Steam power was replaced with electric power. Land companies bought large acreages which were subdivided into small farms suitable for growing alfalfa, grapes, citrus, olives and vegetables, and dairying became a major business.

By 1910, over-planting and over-pumping, coupled with a series of dry years, had depleted the underground water table. In some areas the water that was pumped was so saline that it killed crops. The disaster was gradually lessened by the formation of irrigation districts, better use of water, and a series of wet years. The Central Valley Project, the California Water Plan and dams on the principal rivers have contributed greatly to the solution of the water problem.

The first pumped well for irrigation was dug and put into operation by John J. Cairns on his ranch near Lindsay.

FREMONT TRAIL

John C. Fremont was a conspicuous figure in the conquest of California. No history of western exploration would be complete without a recital of his adventures and mis-adventures.

Fremont came through the valley for the first time in 1844. Tulare Lake was at flood stage and rivers were running bank to bank. Feed was stirrup high. Fremont was a facile writer and he

The Fremont Trail marker at the intersection of highways 65 and 137, west of Lindsay, was moved when the road was relocated. At its present site it stands next to the Butterfield Stage Route marker.

noted in his memoir: "... our road was now one of continued enjoyment; and it was pleasant riding among this assemblage of green pastures with varied flowers and scattered groves, and out of the warm green spring to look at the rocky and snowy peaks where lately we had suffered so much."

On April 9 and 10, 1844, he camped on White River and by April 14 he and his men were out of the valley. As he left Fremont wrote: "One might travel the world over without finding a valley more verdant and fresh, more floral and sylvan, more alive with birds and animals, more bounteously watered than we had left in the San Joaquin."

The Fremont Trail followed or paralleled much of the old Indian trail along the axis of the foothills on the eastern side of the valley. Over the years, that same trail was also called the Emigrant Trail, the Stockton-Los Angeles road, the Butterfield stage route, and Telegraph Road. Some of Fremont's Trail is presently incorporated into Highway 65.

Fremont was a frequent visitor in the lower valley as he traveled to southern California or to the San Emidgo Ranch (now in Kern County), of which he was part owner.

Alta Mira Chapter, Daughters of the American Revolution placed a marker on a portion of the trail west of Lindsay.

FREMONT TRAIL
1845

THIS TABLET MARKS THE TRAIL TAKEN BY GENERAL JOHN CHARLES FREMONT ON HIS FAMOUS MARCH OVER THE ROCKY MOUNTAINS THROUGH CALIFORNIA.

TABLET PLACED BY ALTA MIRA CHAPTER
DAUGHTERS OF THE AMERICAN REVOLUTION
1928

The observant visitor will notice that the date on the tablet should be 1844.

In 1958 State Registered Landmark Number 471 marking a section of the Butterfield stage route west of Lindsay was dedicated by the Tulare County Historical Society. At that time both the Fremont and stage route markers were placed at the intersection of Highway 65 and the Lindsay-Tulare highway.

ROTH'S SPUR

Roth's Spur, now known as Strathmore, came into existence as early as 1878 when John and Peter Roth came to Tulare County from Yolo County. They were joined later by their brothers George, Bennett, Henry and Reinhart and their sisters Mary and Barbara. Mary later married George Limegrover, and Barbara married Owen Flynn.

The Roths dry farmed 3,840 acres of grain between Tule River and the home ranch, which today would be at the intersection of Road 236 and Avenue 200.

When the eastside branch of the Southern Pacific Railroad came through the county in 1888, a grain loading platform was built and called Roth's Spur. When a postoffice was granted in 1896 it was also called Roth postoffice. However, the railroad timetable listed the place as Santos and then Filo instead of Roth's Spur.

In 1900 the Roth brothers sold land to Balfour-Guthrie, an English-owned company which had large investments in warehouses and grain. That company built a warehouse at the Spur platform and also built warehouses in other county communities.

Mrs. Hector Burness, wife of the company manager, named the newly platted townsite Strathmore which she said meant "great valley." The settlers like that name better than either Santos or Filo and in 1907 petitioned successfully to have the name Strathmore given to the community.

ROTH'S SPUR

WHEN JOHN AND PETER ROTH CAME TO TULARE COUNTY IN 1878, THEY ACQUIRED AND DRY FARMED THOUSANDS OF ACRES ALONG THE TULE RIVER, THEIR HOLDINGS EXTENDING NORTH THROUGH THE PRESENT STRATHMORE AREA. IN 1888 THEY BUILT A GRAIN LOADING PLATFORM ON THE WEST SIDE OF THE SOUTHERN PACIFIC TRACKS JUST NORTH OF THIS MARKER. THE SITE BECAME KNOWN AS ROTH'S SPUR. IN 1906 BALFOUR GUTHRIE COMPANY OF LONDON WHO OPERATED THE ROTH RANCH LAID OUT A TOWNSITE AND SUBDIVIDED SURROUNDING ACREAGE INTO SMALL FARMS. THE TOWN WAS KNOWN AS ROTH, BALFOUR, AND FILO BEFORE IT FINALLY BECAME STRATHMORE.

ERECTED BY DOCTOR SAMUEL GREGG GEORGE CHAPTER 1855
E CLAMPUS VITUS
OCTOBER 10, 1981

Smith College was located on what today would be approximately the intersection of D and Elm streets in Tulare. The people in the photograph are members of a double wedding party, December 27, 1887. The couples are on the right side of the picture: James Anderson and Henrietta Pomfret and Charles Littleton and Mary Anderson.

SMITH COLLEGE

Smith College in Tulare was started in 1885 as a branch of the University of Southern California. Its curriculum prepared students to enter that institution as sophomores without taking an examination. Smith College also offered commercial courses for those students who wanted to go into business.

The founder was Dr. William Theodore Frelinghuyson Smith. He came from Illinois and was a graduate of Rush Medical College. Before studying medicine he had been a school teacher.

The college was financed from the sale of land donated by Dr. Smith, Isaac Wright and a Mr. Page. It advertised itself as a nonsectarian college but it was affiliated with the Methodist Church. F. J. Pillsbury was the first principal and J. M. Ward headed the commercial department.

The college was in southeast Tulare and faced north on what today would be the intersection of D and Elm streets. It was housed in a three-story building which included classrooms, a dormitory for girls and a dining hall.

When the Southern Pacific Railroad moved its shops and roundhouse to Bakersfield in 1890 Tulare somehow managed to survive, but Smith College did not. Dr. Smith intended to donate the land on which the college stood for a city park. Although that plan did not materialize, some of the older city maps show the square as Smith Park.

TULARE'S FIRST CHURCH

In the summer of 1872 Lorenzo A. Pratt asked Dr. J. H. Warren, superintendent of home missions in California, to come to Tulare to organize a Congregational Church in the brand new railroad town. At that time, someone had said of Tulare: "There was nothing in sight but land, sky, two T rails and a great future." Dr. Warren and fifteen people, half the population of Tulare, attended the meeting in a small school house.

The Reverend A. L. Rankin was the first pastor. He was a missionary in the truest sense of the word. When he came to Tulare with his wife and four children, the only available house was a small two-room adobe. The Southern Pacific Railroad depot was completed and the pastor was given permission to hold services in the waiting room. The agent was instructed by the railroad to keep the room clean and to do no unnecessary work during church services. Fifteen people promised to come to the first service. No one showed up. The next time nine people came, and the First Congregational Church was organized on November 22, 1874.

The railroad donated land on the corner of I and King streets and the church was formally incorporated November 25, 1875. The new church building was actually built by the Reverend Rankin and was dedicated June 1, 1876. A bell donated to the

The First Congregational Church at 220 West Tulare Street in Tulare.

church by railroad employees rang July 4, 1876, to observe the nation's centennial.

In 1898 the church burned and the congregation met in various halls until a new church was built on the corner of H and West Tulare streets. It was dedicated in February 1900.

TULARE'S FIRST HOUSE

Isaac Wright (1823-1910) sailed to California in 1851 to join his brothers who were mining near Sonora. He left his wife, Charlotte Phillips Wright (1830-1915), in Ohio, promising to come for her as soon as he had made his fortune. Four years went by before he was able to bring her to Sonora.

In a search for farm land, Wright and L. A. Pratt came down into the valley in 1870, to what is now Tulare. Both men were impressed with the country. Isaac Wright pre-empted 160 acres, built a one-room cabin and moved his family to the new location.

The Southern Pacific Railroad reached its newly created town of Tulare in 1872 and officials asked Mr. Wright to trade his property for land directly south. The original parcel became the nucleus of the town of Tulare. When the trade was legally completed, railroad employees helped Wright move his house to the new property. More rooms were added later for the growing family. The house stood at 457 South H Street for more than 100 years. It was razed in the late 1970s.

TULARE LAKE

The phantom Tulare Lake is the oldest historic landmark in the lower valley. There were times when it was the largest fresh water lake west of the Great Lakes. There were times when the lake bed was completely dry, as it is at this writing.

Gabriel Moraga found the lake in 1805 and named it Laguna de los Tulares. He also named the principal contributory river, Rio de los Santos Reyes (Kings River).

Tulare Lake is the natural drainage basin for the Kings, Kaweah and Tule rivers as well as smaller streams south of the Tule. During very wet years overflow water from Kern River and Buena Vista Lake drained into Tulare Lake. The lake bed is 179 feet above sea level. At flood stage it was roughly 448 miles in circumference and the water covered approximately 800 square miles. The lake bed is shallow and the stiff winds of the west side of the valley blew the water out for several miles. Consequently the surrounding land was a marsh overgrown with tules, grass and shrubby trees.

Much of the history of the lower valley revolved around Tulare Lake. Its teeming bird, fish and animal life attracted Indians who developed a distinct lake culture. It was also a rendezvous for trappers, traders, explorers, horse thieves, stockmen, commercial fishermen and farmers.

When the lake water subsided even slightly, islands appeared. The largest had several names. The Indians called it Chaw-loo-win. When stockmen ferried hogs to the island it was called Root Island, and after it was purchased by Visalia attorney A. J. Atwell, it became Atwell's Island. Much of it today is the townsite of Alpaugh. Two smaller islands were Gull and Pelican, named for the birds which inhabited them. Skull Island was five miles long and in some places twenty feet high. Early visitors found human bones and concluded the island was either an Indian burial site or the site of a forgotten battle.

Indians sailed the lake in their remarkable tule boats. Later on, people used barges, fishing boats and pleasure boats. In good weather it took about seven hours to sail around the lake. The stiff winds on its west side often caused boats to capsize or run aground. There were six boat landings: Orton's Point, Gordon's Point, Cox and Clarke Landing, Creighton's Ranch, Rhodes' Landing and Buzzard's Roost, now Waukena.

Irrigation ditches began to divert water from the larger rivers. The terrible dry years of the 1870s took their toll. As the lake water began to subside, adventuresome farmers planted grain in the incredibly fertile soil of the lake bed. Levees were built and often washed away. Crops were washed out but the farmers came back. The lake was completely dry from 1923 until 1937 and immense fields of grain and cotton covered the old lake bed. Special machinery was manufactured to cope with the mammoth crops.

The farmers' battle with water has never ended. In 1937 the lake was full of water. Sail boats and motor boats appeared and fishing was again possible. Gradually, reclamation projects,

Lithograph of the Water Witch *on Tulare Lake in the 1870s.*

drainage projects and better engineered levees made it possible again to use the lake bed for farming. Then in 1969 torrential rains once more brought water into Tulare Lake.

Since Tulare Lake is a natural drainage basin there is always the possibility that it may fill. However, dams on the principal contributing rivers, large scale irrigation and reclamation projects make such an occurrence improbable.

TULARE WOMAN'S CLUB HOUSE

The club house on West Tulare and I streets was built by the Southern Pacific Railroad for its employees. It was called Library Hall since the railroad furnished books for both employees and town people. The building was also a social center, for there was a good-sized stage, and card and billiard tables.

Library Hall was dedicated at a grand ball May 19, 1882. People came from other communities as well and seventy-six couples partook of a sumptuous midnight supper at the Pacific House and then danced until dawn. The ball gown worn by each lady was described in minute detail by the male reporter of the Tulare newspaper.

The railroad created Tulare in 1872 and almost destroyed the community in 1890. That was the devastating year railroad officials moved the shops, the roundhouse and a large payroll to Bakersfield.

In 1896 the City of Tulare was given permission to use the club house for the city library, and it was so used until 1905 when a Carnegie Library was built.

The Tulare Woman's Club was organized in 1912 and the Southern Pacific Railroad turned the building over to the club rent free for maintaining the structure.

Much of Tulare's social history has been made in that club house—entertainments, dances, dinners, weddings, parties, and school graduations. The cost of maintenance grew steadily and in 1969 the railroad agreed to let the Tulare Woman's Club turn the building over to the City of Tulare. The club continues to meet there as do other clubs and agencies.

Tulare Woman's Club House—Library Hall—is located at 88 West Tulare Street in Tulare.

ZUMWALT PARK

This park on the east side of the City of Tulare was renamed Zumwalt Park during Zumwalt Days, April 16-18, 1971. The occasion honored father and son, Dr. Elmo Zumwalt, Sr. and Admiral Elmo Zumwalt, Jr., descendants of John and Mabel Ford Zumwalt, pioneers of Tulare. Dr. Zumwalt (1892-1973) practiced in Tulare for many years. He also served as Tulare City health officer, Tulare County health officer, and as administrator of the Tulare County Hospital. Dr. Zumwalt was elected

The Zumwalt Park marker is on East Tulare Street in Tulare.

mayor of Tulare two times and served for many years on the city school board.

Admiral Zumwalt is a graduate of Annapolis and capped his distinguished naval career by being named the youngest chief of the joint chiefs of staff in the armed services.

The Tulare and M street entrance to the park is marked by a huge concrete anchor and a plaque. The inscription on the plaque reads:

ZUMWALT PARK

IN HONOR OF ELMO R. ZUMWALT, M.D. IN RECOGNITION OF HIS SERVICE TO HIS COMMUNITY AND NATION.

APRIL 17, 1971

The anchor is inscribed:

IN HONOR OF ELMO R. ZUMWALT, JR. IN RECOGNITION OF THE DISTINCTION HE HAS ACHIEVED IN RISING TO THE RANK OF CHIEF OF NAVAL OPERATIONS, UNITED STATES NAVY.

Part 5
Historic Sites in the Northwest Portion of Tulare County

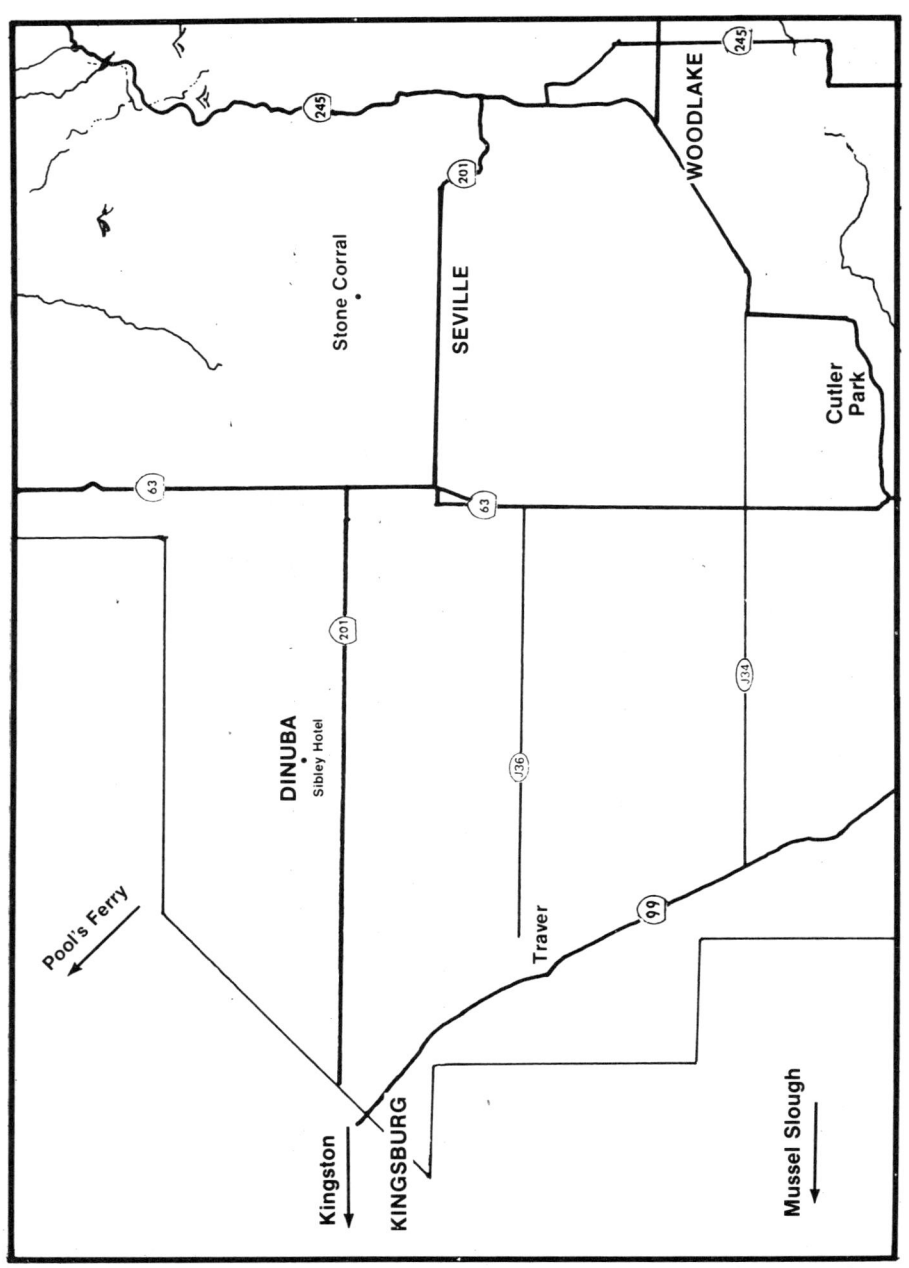

Historic Sites in the Northwest Portion of Tulare County

KINGSTON

Kingston probably will be remembered for a raid made by Tiburcio Vasquez rather than that it was once a thriving settlement, a toll ferry, and a Butterfield stage station.

In 1854, Lucius Whitmore bought and improved the existing ferry on Kings River. The County of Tulare granted him a license the next year and Whitmore's Ferry prospered.

Whitmore had married an Indian woman. In 1859 some local men took it upon themselves to round up any Indians they could find and take them to a reservation. When they came to the ferry, Whitmore defended his family and was murdered. He is buried in the Visalia Cemetery. It is not known what became of his family.

The ferry was a Butterfield stage stop from 1858 until 1861. Then other stage lines used the ferry. The last owner, O. H. Bliss,

Kingston was one and two-tenths miles southwest of Laton on the Kings River.

built a substantial bridge. The name Kingston probably came into use in 1859 when a postoffice was granted to the settlement.

Tiburcio Vasquez was a law-defying daredevil who robbed and committed brutal murders up and down California. On Christmas Eve, 1873, Vasquez, his lieutenant, Chavez, and their gang swooped into Kingston. They tied up thirty men, robbed them, and rifled the safes and tills in the saloons, stores and hotel. They took about twenty-five hundred dollars in cash and an undetermined amount of watches and jewelry. The gang escaped but later it was learned that several of its members were wounded in a gun battle on the bridge. The law finally caught up with Vasquez and he was hanged March 18, 1875 at San Jose.

KINGSTON

FOUNDED IN 1856 BY L. A. WHITMORE WHO OPERATED THE FIRST KINGS RIVER CROSSING. AFTER 1858 TOWN BECAME STOPPING PLACE FOR BUTTERFIELD STAGES. TOLL BRIDGE SUPERCEDED FERRY IN 1873. ON DECEMBER 24, 1873, TIBURCIO VASQUEZ AND BANDIT GANG MADE BOLD RAID ON TOWN ROBBING ENTIRE VILLAGE.

STATE REGISTERED LANDMARK #270
TABLET PLACED BY CALIFORNIA CENTENNIAL COMMISSION
BASE FURNISHED BY KINGS COUNTY CENTENNIAL COMMISSION
DEDICATED FEBRUARY 4, 1950

MUSSEL SLOUGH TRAGEDY

On May 11, 1880, seven men died in an appalling and senseless gun battle that is recorded as the Mussel Slough Tragedy. The story behind that horror is inexorably woven into western railroad history and the anti-monopoly issue that swept the nation a century ago.

The need for a transcontinental railroad was apparent before California came into the Union. The Civil War intensified that need. President Lincoln signed the first of many railroad bills in 1862, providing land and money for a railroad. Eventually the Central Pacific and Union Pacific railroads would receive the odd numbered sections of land on both sides of the track. Money subsidies ranged from $16,000 to $48,000 a mile, depending on the terrain. In return the railroads had to meet completion requirements and other regulatory provisions. The construction of the transcontinental railroad was one of the world's great engineering accomplishments.

No one could foretell the role of the Central Pacific Railroad in California. In an ever-growing welter of graft and corruption, its owners, Charles Crocker, Mark Hopkins, Collis Huntington and Leland Stanford, took over the government of the state. They were best described as being scrupulously dishonest. In order to obtain more land and subsidies, the Big Four absorbed most of the small lines in the state, including the Southern Pacific Railroad.

In 1872 "The Railroad" was built throughout the San Joaquin Valley by the Central Pacific and Southern Pacific lines. Alluring advertisements brought more and more people to California. The population of Tulare County jumped from 4,533 in 1870 to 11,281 in 1880. The land in the southern valley was the best the railroad had to sell to settlers. Brochures promised that settlers could buy railroad land for two and a half dollars an acre and upwards just as soon as the railroad met the requirements in its federal contracts. Improvements made on the farms would not be included in the purchase price. On that promise many people came into an area between the Kings River and Tulare Lake called Mussel Slough or Lucerne Valley. At the time land could be obtained by preemption, homesteading or purchase, so not all settlers were involved in the sales of railroad lands.

People in Lucerne Valley were stunned when railroad land graders appeared and set prices of twenty-five to thirty-five dollars an acre on their farms. They were told that the promise of land "at two and a half dollars an acre and upward" meant exactly what it said. There were constant meetings, trips to Washington, trips to Sacramento, and lawsuits. The litigation went through the California courts and finally to the United States Supreme Court, and every verdict was in favor of the railroad.

Ejection suits began in 1872. If the owner of a farm could not or would not pay the railroad its price, he was summarily ejected and the land was sold. Settlers seemed to be well aware of the presence of land graders so they were usually not at home. The graders would then put the family's possessions out on the road. As soon as they left, neighbors would arrive and help the owners put things back in the house. When the graders caught on to that practice, they began to burn the houses.

People were willing to pay a fair price for land so in 1878 the Settlers Land League was formed in an effort to protect their years of hard work. Tension in Mussel Slough continued to grow. Masked men rode. Threats were sent. Railroad people were asked to leave. The best account of that period is found in Frank Norris's *The Octopus*.

On May 11, 1880, an old fashioned picnic was in progress in Hanford. Some of the men learned that United States Deputy Marshal Alonzo Poole and land grader William Clark were on their way to the Braden ranch to turn it over to two local ranchers, Walter Crow and Mills Hartt. Officials, the new owners of the property and a group of settlers met at the Braden ranch and then rode to the adjoining Brewer ranch three and a half miles northwest of Hanford. The only fact that was later agreed on was that the first shot came from the wagon occupied by Crow and Hartt. In the next few minutes five settlers and two deputy marshals were fatally shot. Walter Crow, who apparently shot most of the men, ran into a wheat field. His body was found the next morning. The inquest jury did not name anyone, but the identity of the man who shot Crow was no secret.

Seventeen men were indicted by a federal grand jury in San Jose for resisting a peace officer in the performance of his duty. Many names had to be dropped from the indictment because the men either had not been at the Brewer ranch or had not been armed. Five men were found guilty, fined $300 each and sentenced to eight months in jail. Their imprisonment in San Jose was one of the oddest in penal history. Most Californians hated the railroad and what it stood for. Anti-monopolists across the nation joined them. The prisoners received money, food and encouragement, and their cells were never locked. The jailor provided living quarters for several of the families. The men attended church and lodge meetings and picked up their mail at the postoffice. When their term was up, the only bachelor among them married the jailor's daughter.

Eventually some compromises were made and a few people were able to buy back their land. Hindsight tells us that while the railroad may have been legally right it was ethically wrong in its treatment of the settlers in Mussel Slough.

The Mussel Slough marker is on Road 14 about four miles north of Grangeville.

MUSSEL SLOUGH

HERE, ON MAY 11, 1880, DURING A DISPUTE OVER LAND TITLES BETWEEN SETTLERS AND RAILROAD, A FIGHT BROKE OUT DURING WHICH SEVEN MEN LOST THEIR LIVES, TWO DEPUTY U.S. MARSHALS AND FIVE RANCHERS. LEGAL STRUGGLES OVER TITLES FINALLY COMPROMISED.

STATE REGISTERED LANDMARK #245

TABLET FURNISHED BY CALIFORNIA CENTENNIALS COMMISSION
BASE FURNISHED BY KINGS COUNTY HISTORICAL SOCIETY
DEDICATED FEBRUARY 4, 1948

POOL'S FERRY

Pool's Ferry on the Kings River is one of the most historic but least known landmarks in the lower valley. It had at least two locations and the name is sometimes spelled Poole's Ferry.

The owners, John Pool, B. F. Edmunds and W. J. Campbell, were the first settlers in Tulare County, predating the Woods party by a few months. All three voted in the 1852 organization election of the county, and Pool was elected to the Board of Supervisors in 1853.

The first location of the ferry and trading post was about a mile east of Centerville. The trading post was on a sand bar in the Kings River which bore the inappropriate name of Grand Island. A rancheria was nearby. That site was used until the high water of 1852 forced the owners to move it about two miles north of present Reedley at what is now called Reedley Narrows. The ferry was actually a large barge operated by block and tackle. When the river was full or swift or both the expense of using the ferry was worth the time saved.

In 1855 James Smith built a ferry five miles downstream in a better location and absorbed Pool's ferry business. The next year Pool moved to Mendocino County. Edmunds disappeared from our recorded history. William J. Campbell served as an Indian agent and later became a cattleman in both Tulare and Kern counties.

Pool's first ferry, which was within the reservation created by federal treaties, was the locale of dramatic events in the history of Tulare County. Grand Island was one of the polling places for the organizational election, July 10, 1852. A few days earlier a posse of Americans made an unwarranted raid on the nearby rancheria and killed a number of Indians. The raid was so unjust that it was condemned in the state press, an unusual event in California at the time.

Walter Harvey, leader of the raiders, was elected judge of Tulare County on July 10. A month later he was in the limelight again.

Major James Savage had been appointed by the legislature to head the commission which organized Tulare County. He had arrived in California in 1846, joined Fremont's California Battalion, worked for John Sutter, and then disappeared into the San Joaquin Valley, where he emerged as El Rey Tulares, leader of several Indian tribes. He set up trading posts and did a lucrative business with the Indians. When the Mariposa Indian War (1851-1852) broke out he was selected to lead the Mariposa Battalion which eventually subdued the Indians. After the war he regained the confidence of the Indians and returned to trading.

Savage had quarrelled openly with Harvey over the treatment of the Indians. In the middle of August, Savage was on his way to Woodsville to hold a talk with the Indians. He met Harvey at Pool's Ferry where they argued and fought. In the melee, Harvey shot and killed Savage. His remains were buried by Pool's Ferry but were later taken to his Fresno River trading post. In 1971 a reclamation project made it necessary to move Savage's grave, which is now in the City of Madera.

SIBLEY HOTEL

James Sibley and his brothers-in-law, Edward Giddings, Reed Giddings and C. F. Giddings, came to the 76 country in 1883. Together they bought all of Section 21 T 16 R 24. Sibley and Edward Giddings bought the northwest quarter of Section 18 T 16 R 24. Giddings sold his interest in that parcel to W. D. Tuxbury. In a few years it would be the site of the new railroad town of Dinuba.

Tuxbury was not a newcomer as he was a partner in the warehouse firm of Kitchner and Tuxbury in Cross Creek, a small, busy village that would later be absorbed by Traver and Dinuba.

Tuxbury and Sibley hired three well-known local carpenters to build a hotel. The men, Abner Fraser, W. F. McCracken and E. E. McCracken, built an imposing two-story hotel on what today is the corner of Kern and L streets. On the lower floor were the hotel office, a drug store, a saloon, dining room, the kitchen, and sample rooms for drummers. Tuxbury named the hotel for his partner. It was leased to Mr. and Mrs. Henry Kirkpatrick. Ten years later, the hotel was destroyed by fire.

Sibley Hotel, located on the corner of present Kern and L streets in Dinuba.

The eastside railroad came through the valley in 1887-88. Tuxbury and Sibley deeded acreage to the Pacific Improvement Company, the real estate branch of the Southern Pacific Railroad, and Dinuba was born.

The derivation of the name Dinuba remains an enigma. The first name of the community was Sibleyville. That was shortened to Sibley, but when the railroad timetable was printed the name was Dinuba and that name was given to the postoffice which was established on February 9, 1889. The meaning of the name has never been explained satisfactorily.

SMITH'S FERRY AND SMITH MOUNTAIN CEMETERY

James Smith (1821-1862) established his ferry in 1855 in what is now the southwest section of Reedley. The location on the high banks of the Kings River made it easier to approach the ferry in times of high water. It was also possible for Smith to see and be ready for approaching teams. Smith rapidly absorbed much of Pool's Ferry business.

The ferry was a sixteen- by sixty-foot barge. The two loading platforms were hinged so they could be attached to the ferry, which was operated by block and tackle tied to heavy timber. Smith placed the cables high so driftwood would not snag against them. The ferry cost $2,000 and the cables cost $500.

The nearby Smith home doubled as a hotel. It was a two-story building with eleven rooms and like the ferry was made from lumber hauled from Thomas's Mill east of Visalia.

The franchise granted by Tulare County to collect tolls was the same as that granted earlier to John Pool. Smith's books show that he did an excellent business.

In 1861 James Smith was elected to the California State Legislature but he did not live to complete his term. He and his son William contracted pneumonia and they both died in 1862. They are buried on the bluff overlooking the ferry site in what is now Smith Mountain Cemetery.

His widow, Martha, and their son Hamilton continued to operate the ferry and hotel until 1874 when they sold to J. W.

Mitchell and W. E. Ross. Eventually the property was bought by the 76 Land and Water Company. The old ferry had washed downstream and in 1886 the hotel was dismantled and the lumber was used at a camp near Watoka Dam.

STONE CORRAL

This is the oldest man-made landmark in Tulare County. It is located on the southeast side of Stokes Mountain east of Cutler and northeast of Seville. James Smith (not the James Smith of Smith's Ferry) built the corral in 1853. He piled up the rocks to make an enclosure roughly fifty feet in diameter and used it as a pen for his hogs.

Stone Corral became famous for something else. Dr. Samuel Gregg George Chapter of E Clampus Vitus placed a marker which tells the story. The marker is by the office of the Stone Corral Irrigation District, not at the corral itself.

STONE CORRAL

PERHAPS AS EARLY AS 1853, JAMES SMITH BUILT A STONE CORRAL FOR HIS HOGS ABOUT TWO MILES NORTH OF HERE ON THE LOWER SLOPE OF STOKES MOUNTAIN.

IT BECAME A LANDMARK WHEN, ON JUNE 11, 1893, A SHERIFF'S POSSE SHOT IT OUT WITH THE NOTORIOUS BADMEN, JOHN SONTAG AND CHRIS EVANS, WOUNDING SONTAG FATALLY AND EVANS SERIOUSLY.

DR. SAMUEL GREGG GEORGE CHAPTER 1855
E CLAMPUS VITUS
OCTOBER 11, 1975

The remains of the corral, shown in photograph to the left, are on the southeast slope of Stokes Mountain near Orosi.

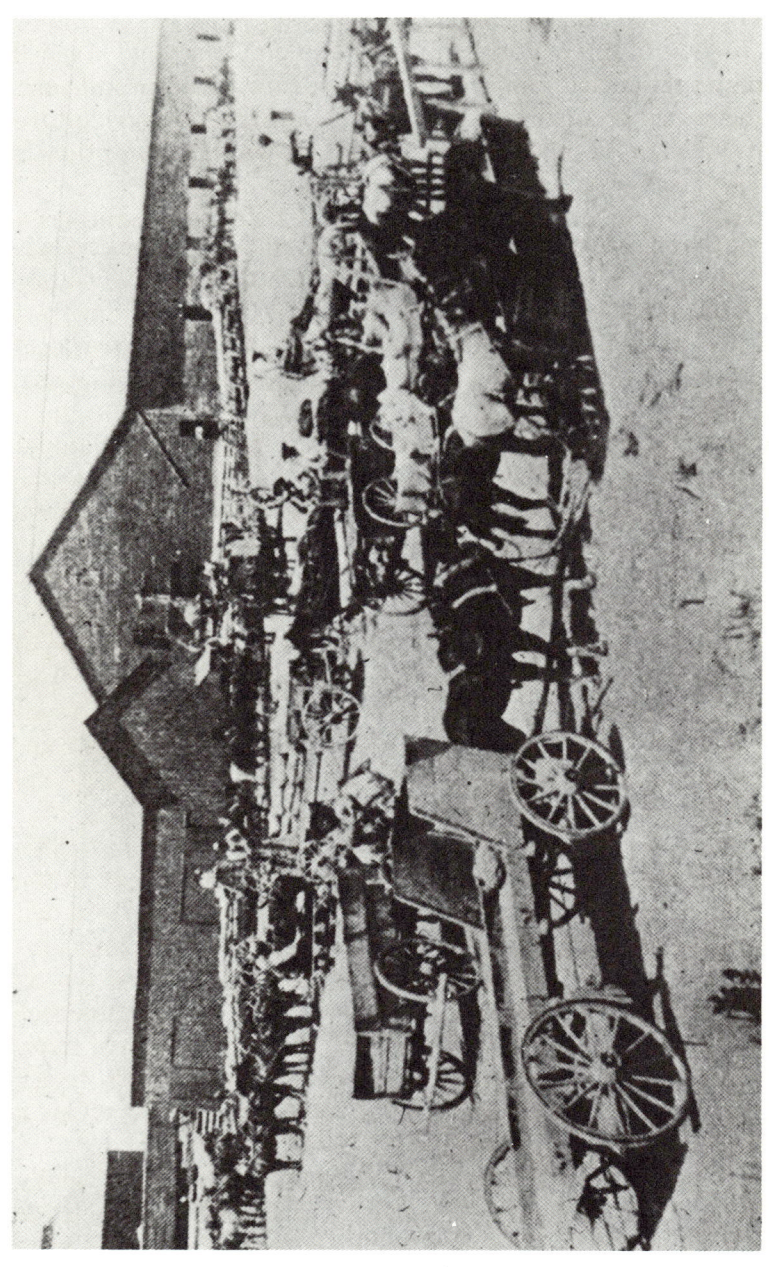

Unloading grain at Traver in 1890.

TRAVER

Many California mining camps had a history of boom and bust, ending up as ghost towns, but few towns based on agriculture went through such distressing experiences. An exception is Traver, now on its way back from ghost town status.

Traver began when men of foresight realized that farming on the valley floor had to be implemented with dependable irrigation water. Peter Y. Baker, an engineer, conceived a project which would divert water from the Kings River. In 1882 his project became the 76 Land and Water Company, which optioned 130,000 acres in northern Tulare and southern Fresno counties. The company took its name from the 76 country which in turn had taken its name from Senator Thomas Fowler's "76" cattle brand. The cattle baron of the valley, at times Fowler ran 200,000 head of cattle on his various rangelands. Although he was a director of the 76 Land and Water Company, which has optioned much of his rangeland, the town planned for the venture was named for another director, Charles Traver.

The key to the entire irrigation project was the construction of the 76 Canal, later called the Alta Canal. Traver was surveyed into town lots and the surrounding land was platted for small farms. Water rights went with the land. Advertisements appeared in city newspapers and the railroad supplied excursion trains for prospective buyers.

The first water flowed through the canal in December 1883, but the headgates had to be closed for repair of a break in the canal bank. When the first contingent of buyers arrived on April 8, 1884, water was flowing through the canal. On that auspicious day the depot was the only completely finished building but by the end of the day buyers had invested $65,000. Two months later Traver had two general stores, a drug store, a hardware store, two lumber yards, two hotels, two barber shops, two livery stables, three saloons, a postoffice, a school, an express office, a large Chinatown and a lively red light district.

Fruit, grapes, vegetables and alfalfa did well, but basically Traver was a storage and shipping point for grain. Each of three warehouses held 30,000 tons of sacked grain. Most of the time

Traver marker may be seen in Traver Park.

they were filled and sacks of grain were piled outside and along the railroad right of way. Teamsters waited hours and even days to unload their wagons. By 1886 Traver was one of the largest grain shipping towns in the nation.

Traver's decline began in the midst of its prosperity. There was a series of devastating fires. In 1888 the eastside railroad created the towns of Reedley, Dinuba, Cutler, Orosi and Monson, which competed for Traver's business. Fires and new communities were not the only factors; Traver was ruined by the same thing which created it—water. The soil was alkaline and natural rainfall had never penetrated to any depth. Heavy irrigation percolated patches of alkali to the surface and made the soil unfit for farming.

Businessmen began to move to the new towns. Farmers had much more to lose. The 76 Land and Water Company, its stockholders, and remaining tenants were involved in long and expensive litigation over water rights. The company was dissolved in 1945 but long before that year the Alta Irrigation District had taken over the vast irrigation project.

Today, scientific farming methods have restored much of the

land to productivity, and Traver seems to be on its way back as a community. Its importance to many is emphasized every year on April 8 when descendants of early settlers come back for a Traver Day Homecoming.

TRAVER

TRAVER TOWNSITE WAS LAID OUT BY THE 76 LAND AND WATER COMPANY. AN AUCTION OF LOTS WAS HELD APRIL 8, 1884. WITHIN SIXTY DAYS A SMALL TOWN WAS IN EXISTENCE. IT PROSPERED FOR A FEW YEARS AND WAS PROBABLY THE LARGEST GRAIN SHIPPING POINT IN THE UNITED STATES. IRRIGATION CAUSED THE ALKALI TO COME TO THE SURFACE IN THE AREA NEARBY AND THE LAND BECAME WORTHLESS. CONSTRUCTION OF THE EAST-SIDE BRANCH OF THE SOUTHERN PACIFIC DIVERTED FREIGHT TO REEDLEY AND DINUBA.

THE 76 COMPANY SOLD ITS CANALS AND WATER RIGHTS TO THE ALTA IRRIGATION DISTRICT IN 1890. TRAVER ALMOST DISAPPEARED.

DR. SAMUEL GREGG GEORGE CHAPTER 1855
E CLAMPUS VITUS

OCTOBER 3, 1974

Index

Abbey, Arthur, 99, 101
Academy of the Nativity, 28
Advance, 61
Allensworth, 121, 122
Allensworth, Allen, 121, 122
Alpaugh, 136
Alta Canal, 157
Alta Vista School, 110-12
Anderson, George, 57
Artesian Wells, 122, 123
Ash Mountain, 52
Atwell, Allen J., 136
Atwell Island, 136

Baker, Mrs. Lucretia, 41
Baker, Nathan, 12
Baker, Peter Y., 157
Baker, Thomas, 12, 15
Balch, Mr. and Mrs. A. C., 73
Balch Park, 73, 74, 78, 88, 91
Bartlett Park, 73, 74
Bartlett, William P., 57, 73, 74
Battle Mountain, 75, 76
Beale, Edward F., 110
Bell, General Tyree, 17
Belnap, Charles, 111
Bennett, A. A., 37
Berry, George S., 124-26
Berry Harvester, 124-26
Bicentennial Tree, 77
Biggs, Dewitt C., 108
Blair, Rev. Jonathan, 64
Bliss, O. H., 145
Board of Forestry, 54, 57, 58, 74
Bohnert, Augustus, 69
Bonsall Murders, 111
Boothill, 78, 80, 81, 109
Borglum, Solon, 58
Braly, Shade, 84
Braden Ranch, 148
Bravo Lake, 64
Brown, Clinton, 88
Brown, Samuel C., 12, 20
Bubble Tower, 67
Buckman, Carol, 50, 51
Buckman, Dr. Phillip, 50, 51
Burbank Park, 100
Butterfield, John, 3
Butterfield Stations, 3-8, 96, 103, 130, 131, 145

Cahoon, George, 53
Cairns, John J., 65, 128, 129
California Hot Springs, 107
Camp Babbitt, 14-17, 84
Camp Lena, 87
Campbell, David, 98, 113
Campbell, William J., 12, 150
Carothers, Nellie, 99
Carpenter, Isaac, 25
Carroll, Ralph, 112
Carson, Kit, 96
Cartmill, Mary, 126-28
Cartmill, Dr. William, 126-28
Cartmill, W. B., 126
Cenotaph, 31
Centennial Stump, 81
Centennial Tree, 31, 32
Chatten, Richard, 12
Chescott, 81
Chicago Tree (General Noble), 43
Chief Chappo, 51

Chief Francisco, 40
churches, 21, 22, 98, 134
Civil War, 14-17, 146
Clark, Henry, 101
Clark, William, 148
Coburn, Avon, 107
Cottonwood Hotel, 65
Court Houses, 26, 35, 37, 40
Cowden, Henry, 47
Crabtree, John, 107
Crabtree Springs, 107
Cromley, Aaron, 122
Cross Creek Station, 7, 151
Crow, Walter, 148
Crowley, James, 56
Crowley, John, 22
Cutler, 38
Cutler, Dr. John, 12, 37, 75
Cutler Park, 37

Dade, Father Daniel Francis, 28
Daughters of the American Revolution, 56, 131
Daugherty, Dan, 79
Daunt, 107
Daunt, William, 107
Davenport, Dr. William, 22
DeMasters, Foster, 75
Dennis, John, 84
Dillon, Nathan, 67
Dogtown, 108
Doty, A. J., 73
Douglass, David R., 18
Douglass Tree, 18
Doyle, John J., 73, 88
Ducor, 78, 83, 84, 108
Duncan, O. H. P., 107
Dutch Corners, 83, 84

Edmunds, B. F., 150
Election Tree, 38-41
Elkhorn, 7
"End of the Trail," 55, 58, 59
Equal Rights Expositor, 15
Evans, Col. George, 15
Everton, Alfred, 53
Exeter, 99

Filo, 132
Firebaugh Ferry, 7
Firebaugh, John, 69
Fisher, Rev. O. P., 22
Fleck, Henry, 99, 101
flour mills, 67, 99-101
Flynn, Mr. and Mrs. Owen, 132
Fort Tejon, 3, 6
Fort Visalia, 11-14
Fountain Springs, 4, 95
Fowler Switch, 157
Fowler, Thomas, 157
Frame, Howard, 104
Fraser, Abner, 151
Fraser, James E., 58
Fremont, John C., 96, 130, 131, 151
Fremont Trail, 130, 131
Fresno City, 7
Fresno Scraper, 124
Fry, Waltr, 46

Garces, Father Francisco, 109
General Grant Tree, 41
General Noble Tree, 43

160

General Sherman Tree, 45
George, Alan, 13
George, Dr. Samuel G., 74, 75, 86, 111
Giant Forest, 53
Gibbons, Mr. and Mrs. D. G., 85, 113
Giddings Brothers, 151
Glenn, Alex, 12
Glenn, Richard, 12
Goad, John, 40
Goodhue, Peter, 5
Gordon Ferry, 4
Gordon, Jack, 79
Grand Island, 150
Gross, Theodore, 62
Groupie, Samuel, 79

Hambright, J. M., 46
Hamilton, Lester, 104
Hammond, Mrs. John H., 73
Harris, Ben, 46, 47
Hartt, Mills, 148
Harvey, Walter, 150
Henry, Albert, 101
Henry, Willshire, 101
Hercules Tree, 87
Hilliard, Abraham, 40
Hirshady, Fred, 62
Hockett, John, 47
Hockett Trail, 47
Hoffman, George, 111
Hog Wallows, 48
Homer, Rodney, 85
Hoskins, Jesse, 87
Hospital Rock, 51
hotels, 22, 65, 66, 152
Hubbard, Henry, 60, 62
Hunsaker, Henry, 100

Indian Rock Basins, 89

Jacob, Elias, 110
Jacob, Morphew, 54
Jacob, Thomas, 54
James, David, 108
Jeske, Byron, 27
Jones, Thomas, 81
Johnston, L. A., 22
Johnson, J. Sub, 22
Johnston, T. P., 101
Jordan, John, 91, 146, 147
Jordan, Silas, 91
Jordan Trail, 15, 91, 94
Jordan Tree, 91
Jordan, William, 91

Kaweah Colony, 60
Kaweah Post Office, 60
Keener, John, 12, 28
Keeney, J. P., 99, 101
Keller, Charles, 28, 62
Keyes Mine, 108
King, Clarence, 48
Kings County, 103, 104
Kingston, 145, 146
Kirkpatrick, Mr. and Mrs. Henry, 151

Lane, Danny, 79
Lantrip, Erma, 125
Lantrip, Karen, 125
Lemon Cove, 47, 64, 65
Leslie, Andrew, 100, 101

Leslie, Dr. W. W., 101
Lewis, Isaac, 67
Limegrover, Mr. and Mrs. George, 132
Lime Kiln, 65
Lindsay, 7, 65, 128, 129
Lindsay Land Company, 65
Lindsey, Tipton, 20
Little White Schoolhouse, 25-27
Logsdon, James, 112
Lone Cottonwood Station, 6, 103
Lone Oak Cemetery, 55
Loyd, John, 111
Lucerne Valley, 146, 147
lynchings, 26, 111
Lyons, Early, 12

McCracken, E. E., 151
McCracken, W. F., 151
McCrory, James, 26
McKelvey, George, 99
McKelvey, Mr. and Mrs. John, 99
McKelvey, Rev. John, 22, 99
McKelvey, J. Addison, 99
McLean, Charles, 99
Madden Farm, 110
Madden, Thomas, 110
magnesite mines, 74
Maltby, A. J., 108
Maltby, Charles, 111
Manter, John, 101
Manter, Hiram, 101
Mapes, Andrew, 99
Mariposa Indian War, 35, 75, 151
Mark Twain Tree, 63
Martin, James, 98
Martin, Lyman, 47
Martin, William, 113
Mason-Henry Gang, 15, 79
Matthews Brothers, 11, 12, 99
Matthews Mill, 12
May, Mrs. Viva, 62
Memorial Park, 31
Mickley, J. J., 12
Mills, 11, 19, 67, 75, 99-101
Mitchell, Levi, 81, 108
Monson, 64
Montgomery, Mrs. Nora, 64, 65
Mooney Grove, 54, 56, 58, 74
Mooney, Hugh, 7, 58, 59
Moraga, Gabriel, 136
Mount Whitney Power and Electric, 73
Mountain Home, 73
Mountain Home State Forest, 81, 82, 89
Mountain House Station, 4
Murray, Abraham, 12
Murray, George, 100, 101
Murray, J. Patrick, 99-101
Murray Park, 100
Mussel Slough, 146-49

Nelson, John, 67
newspapers, 15, 25

Old Stage Road, 95
Ormsby, William, 3, 4, 6

Packwood Station, 6, 103
Paige and Morton Ranch, 122
Parker, John, 81
Patterson, John, 12
Payne, Dr. Thomas, 40

Persian, James, 22
Pike Lawless Station, 6
Pillsbury, F. J., 134
"The Pioneer," 55, 58
Pioneer Land Company, 100
Plano, 96, 97, 107, 113
Poer, Dan, 79
Pogue, J. W. C., 64, 65
Pogue Hotel, 65
Poindexter, William, 75
Pool, John, 150, 151
Pool's Ferry, 150, 151
Poole, Alonzo, 148
Porterville's first church, 98
Porterville Flour Mill, 99
post offices, 3, 107, 108, 113
Pratt, Lorenzo, 134, 135
Prestage, L. E., 85
pumped wells, 128, 129
Purdy, Mrs. Ida, 62
Putnam, R. Porter, 5, 103-5

Rancho De Kaweah, 65
Rankin, Rev. A. L., 134
Reedley Narrows, 150
Reynolds, Edgar, 11
Reynolds, James, 37
Righter, J. W., 84
Roberts, Calhoun, 12
Robinson, Jerry, 79
Roth family, 132
Roth Spur, 132
Ruiz, Francisco, 56
Russell, Harvey, 67
Russell, Dr. W. G., 35

San Emidgo, 131
San Joaquin Rolling Mill, 67
Santos, 132
Savage, James, 40, 41, 110, 151
schools, 20, 26, 28, 110-15
Schultz, Mrs. Hannah, 117
Sebastian Reserve, 110
Sequoia National Park, 43, 53
Settlers Land League, 148
76 Land and Water Company, 155, 157
Shannon, John, 25
Ship, George, 12
Shoup, S. R., 84
Sibley, 153
Sibley Hotel, 151, 152
Sibley, James, 151
Sibleyville, 153
Smith College, 133, 134
Smith Ferry, 153-55
Smith, James, 155
Smith, James, 150, 153, 154
Smith, Jedediah, 96
Smith Mountain Cemetery, 153
Smith, Peg-Leg, 96
Smith, Orson K., 3, 75
Smith, Dr. W. T. F., 133
Soda Springs, 105-7
Solita, 121
Sontag and Evans, 155
Springville, 105-7
Stevenson, Robert, 12
Stewart, Colonel George, 76, 89
Stiner, Miss Ina, 104, 107, 108
Stone Corral, 155, 156

Strathmore, 6, 63
Street, Garrett, 12
Summer Home, 73
Swanson, John, 53
Sweet, Solomon, 30, 107

Tailholt, 78, 108-10
Taylor, Rev. B. W., 28
Taylor, Horace, 62
Tejon Pass, 110
Tharp, Hale, 51, 53
Thompson, William, 112
Three Rivers, 51
Tibbens, Charles, 84
Tipton, 122
Traver, 157-59
Traver, Charles, 157
Travis, J. D., 26
Tree Ranch, 122
Tucker, Cage, 111
Tulare's first church, 134
Tulare's first houses, 126, 127, 135, 136
Tulare Lake, 136-38
Tulare Woman's Club House, 138, 139
Tule River Indian Reservation, 76, 110-12
Tule River Indian War, 76, 110
Tule River School District, 112
Tule River Stage Station, 5, 103
Tuxbury, W. D., 151
Tyler, John, 99, 112

Utley, James, 81

Vandalia, 96, 103, 113, 114
Vasquez, Tiburcio, 145, 146
Vincent, Earl, 66
Vincent, Kenneth, 66
Vise, Nathaniel, 12, 13
Vivian, Thomas, 32, 81
Vivian, William, 32, 81
Vosburg, Joel, 111

Walker, Joseph R., 96
Ward, J. M., 134
Warren, Dr. J. H., 134
Waukena, 123, 137
Webb, Dr. John, 22
Weckert, John, 62
Wells, James, 15
Wells, Matt, 79
Whaley, Dr. Franklin, 112
White, Huffum, 110, 111
White River, 78, 108-10
Whitmore Ferry, 7, 145
Whitmore, Lucius, 7, 145
Wilcox, Origen, 112
Williams, John W., 112
Willis, Benjamin, 57
Willis, Thomas, 12
Wolverton, James, 46
Worthington, Peter, 79
Woods, John, 35, 38, 40
Woodsville, 3, 11, 16, 35, 38-41, 55
Woodville, 114, 115
Wright, Isaac, 133, 135

Zalud House, 115
Zalvidea, Jose, 56, 60
Zumwalt Park, 140, 141